An introduction to APL

Cambridge Computer Science Texts · 17

An introduction to APL

S. POMMIER
Collective name for a team at the Ecole Nationale Supérieure des Mines comprising:
Jean-Jacques Girardot
Serge Guiboud-Ribaud
Bertrand Jullien
Francois Mireaux
Michel Nakache

Translated by Bronwen A. Rees

CAMBRIDGE UNIVERSITY PRESS
Cambridge
London New York New Rochelle
Melbourne Sydney

Published by the Press Syndicate of the University of Cambridge
The Pitt Building, Trumpington Street, Cambridge CB2 1RP
32 East 57th Street, New York, NY 10022, USA
296 Beaconsfield Parade, Middle Park, Melbourne 3206, Australia

Originally published in French as *Introduction à APL* by
Dundod informatique, Paris and © BORDAS, Paris, 1978
First published in English by Cambridge University Press 1983 as
An introduction to APL
English edition © Cambridge University Press 1983

Printed in Great Britain at the University Press, Cambridge

Library of Congress catalogue card number: 83-7374

British Library cataloguing in publication data

Pommier, S.
An introduction to APL – (Cambridge computer science texts; 17)

1. APL (Computer program language)
I. Title II. Rees, B. A.
III. Introduction à APL. English
001.64′24   QA76.72.A27

ISBN 0 521 24977 5 hard covers
ISBN 0 521 27109 6 paperback

DJ

CONTENTS

PREFACE

APL originates from the work of K. E. Iverson, during his time as Professor at Harvard, on formalising algorithms. Its fundamental concepts are outlined in his book, *A Programming Language*, published in 1962. It was first used on a computer at IBM in the late 1960s.

The Department of Computer Science of the Ecole des Mines at Saint-Etienne developed several APL systems. In recent years new APL systems have been appearing and the use of the language is beginning to spread.

The present manual is designed to guide the first steps of the APL user. Consequently, only those aspects which we believe to be essential for a graded study in computer science have been detailed – the reader will not find an APL reference manual for a specific computer here. Numerous examples have been given to illustrate the text. They have been programmed on our system and the responses shown are those that actually occurred. We have tried our best to avoid particular cases, but where this has been impossible we have informed the reader in a footnote. In order to help the reader two appendices appear at the end of the text:

> The current APL alphabet,
> An APL mini-guide.

1 INTRODUCING THE TERMINAL

1.1 From slide rule to APL

The last few years have witnessed the development of more and more sophisticated methods of calculation.

Just as the slide rule has become a museum piece, pocket calculators which could only carry out a few operations have been superseded by pocket micro-computers, capable of being programmed in a developed language. Nevertheless, these machines still have their limitations, particularly in their capacity for storing data. The moment one needs to carry out operations of any significant size, it becomes necessary to use a 'true computer' the size of which is decreasing from year to year if not from month to month. Which language should be used? Without doubt, because of its power and (debugging) capabilities, APL is one of the most useful. It is now available on a wide range of computers from the very large to the very small.

To work in APL then, it is necessary to have access to a computer capable of understanding the language, that is, capable of understanding or executing the calculations demanded of it by the language user. In this chapter we shall examine how the APL machine can be used. We shall call it indiscriminately the APL interpreter or system.

1.2 The terminal and the computer

In order to make use of the computer's ability to perform calculations rapidly, we obviously must be able to transmit the necessary instructions to it. For this a *terminal* (sometimes called a *console*) is used. A terminal consists of a keyboard, similar to that of a typewriter. Through this keyboard the user instructs the computer. In addition, part of the terminal is designed for the computer to communicate results (or other information) to the user, in response to instructions he has given. The technology of this part, the 'output device', varies according to the terminal model.

Generally, they are of two types: a visual display unit (like a television screen), or a line printer that prints on paper (like a typewriter). However, the answer supplied by the computer is independent of the type of terminal used.

The terminal is either linked to the computer directly of via a telephone line depending on where it is situated. The data typed in by the user on the terminal is sent to the computer which subsequently communicates the result.

1.3   Entering instructions

Each character entered on the keyboard is transmitted to the computer which then displays the character on the screen (or piece of paper). The computer must be told when a line (also called an *instruction*) has been completed and this is done by depressing the 'carriage return' key. This indicates that it is now (and only now) that the computer should execute the calculation demanded of it. The carriage (or cursor if using a screen†) then moves to the beginning of the next line. We shall see later how to correct typing errors.

Unfortunately, different keyboards are not all identical and the reader should try to familiarise himself with each of them. Figure 1 gives an example of one. On the majority of keyboards, certain keys represent up to four characters (see Figure 2). In APL only the characters situated on the left hand side are used. To enter the characters situated in the upper part of the left hand side the relevant

† It is only through linguistic misuse that we still tend to use the term 'carriage'. This can refer to either carriage or cursor depending on the type of terminal used.

Figure 1

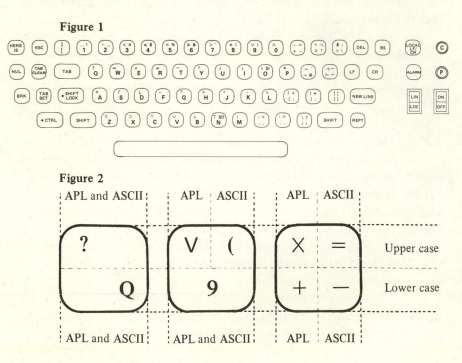

Figure 2

¦ APL and ASCII ¦	¦ APL ¦ ASCII ¦	¦ APL ¦ ASCII ¦	
?	∨ (	× =	Upper case
Q	9	+ —	Lower case
¦ APL and ASCII ¦	¦ APL and ASCII ¦	¦ APL ¦ ASCII ¦	

key and the shift key should be struck simultaneously. A special selector, APL/ ASCII, makes the choice between characters on the right or left. The set of characters available in APL is the same whatever the terminal used:

> 0123456789 *ABCDEFGHIJKLMNOPQRSTUVWXYZ* ( ) [ ]
> +−×÷∗○⌈⌊|<≤=≠≥>∧∨~ αειρω?¨‾↑→↓←⊃∩∪⊂⊥ ⊤ .,:;/\□'○∆⍋

1.4   The computer's reply

When the calculation has been completed, the computer prints the result at the terminal and awaits further instruction on the next line, having shifted the carriage six spaces to the right.

An APL instruction often consists of no more than a few characters, but it can, on the other hand, take up more than one line of the terminal (in the physical sense). Equally, an instruction might simply consist of 'carriage return' to move to the following line.

1.5   APL expressions

A simple APL expression might consist of a single number or of two numbers separated by a function, thus:

```
      6
6
```

```
      3×5
15
```

Numbers are expressed in decimal form; if any part of the number is a fraction, it is separated from the integer part by a decimal point. The integer or the fractional part can be omitted if it is equal to zero. For example:

```
      .5+2.75
3.25
```

```
      1.7+2.3
4
```

Results supplied by the computer are printed following the same convention. In particular, the fractional part of a result will only be indicated if not equal to zero. But, for example, the terms 3, 3. and 3.00 are equivalent.

We have all used certain functions of the APL system from a very tender age. These are addition, subtraction, multiplication and division, represented by the keys +, −, ×, and ÷. These functions, used to carry out the majority of everyday numerical calculations, are called dyadic because two operands are necessary.

Thus:

```
        2×3
6
        1521+873
2394
```

```
        7865÷715
11
        605-872
⁻267
```

In this example a new sign ⁻ appears which indicates that the number is negative. Let us try using it:

```
        ⁻1
⁻1
```

```
        -1
⁻1
```

The machine obstinately yields the result ⁻1. Does this mean that the two keys — and ⁻ have the same effect? In reality, no. In the first instance, — is the unary function (also called the *monadic* function) which, when applied to a number, gives its opposite value. In the second case, the expression is composed of the single constant, 'minus one'. The sign ⁻ is a symbol used to represent negative numerical constants.

Also, this example shows us how a symbol such as — can have two distinct functions, depending on whether it is applied to a single number (or, more generally, operand) or to two. This is true for the majority of symbols used in APL. Let us try to discover the meanings of the other monadic functions corresponding to the keys +, ×, and ÷:

```
        +5
5
        +⁻8
⁻8
        ×5
1
```

```
        ×2
1
        ×⁻3
⁻1
        ×0
0
```

We can see that the × key, when used in its monadic form, gives the sign of its operand: 1 if positive, 0 if zero, and ⁻1 if negative. Let us continue our investigation:

```
        ÷2
.5
        ÷3
.333333
        ÷ ⁻1
⁻1


        ÷0
DOMAIN ERROR
        ÷0
        ∧
```

This is rather a strange reaction from a machine that until now has proved to be quite amenable. It is, in fact, quite simply, an 'error message'. The machine is not capable of executing a division by zero. As the machine indicates, we have left the *domain* of the definition of the function used (in this case, the function of division).

Furthermore, the symbol ∧ shows precisely where the error lies, which is very useful when we have a long expression comprising several functions.

1.6 Exponential notation

Let us calculate:

```
        12300×27200
3.3456E8
```

In giving the answer, the machine adopts a neat notation: E8 means 'multiplied by 10 to the power of 8'. This representation is always used when the answer moves outside the domain in which the usual notation is clearer. Thus the computer will print 125 or 0.23, and not 1.25E2 or 2.3E⁻1, but 1.3E9 or 3.65E⁻11 and not 1300000000 or 0.0000000000365. However, in an expression, the terms 1E5 and 100000, for example, are strictly equivalent.

1.7 Error messages

Generally speaking, an error message indicates that the computer finds it impossible to execute a task properly. One of the more common reasons might be a mathematical impossibility:

```
        3÷0
DOMAIN ERROR
        3÷0
        ∧
```

Another cause might be the machine's limitations. For example:

```
      1.234E567
LIMIT ERROR
      1.234E567
      ∧
```

In fact, the internal specification for the representation of numbers means that they must lie within a certain interval, for example:

$$[^-1.701411E38 \quad 1.701411E38]$$

this interval varying from one computer to another.

Such an error, generally called a *'limit error'*, can also occur in any intermediate calculation:

```
      1E20×3.5E30
LIMIT ERROR
      1E20×3.5E30
          ∧
```

Other errors may result from the incorrect format for a number being used. For example:

```
      ‾ 125
SYNTAX ERROR
      ‾ 125
      ∧
      1 . 5E 4
SYNTAX ERROR
      1 . 5E 4
          ∧
```

In fact, spaces are not allowed between the negative sign and the number, or within the number itself or the exponent.

Another type of error occurs when an expression does not mean anything to the computer. For example:

```
      1+
SYNTAX ERROR
      1+
      ∧
```

1.8   Some other APL functions

(*a*)   *Power and exponential*
These functions are symbolised by the key * which in its monadic form represents the exponential, and, in its dyadic form, a power.

```
      3*2
9
      4*3
64
```

A power can also be a fraction or a negative number:

```
      2*.5
1.41421
      4*⁻1.5
.125
```

As stated in its monadic form, the symbol represents the exponential:

```
      *1
2.71828
```

```
      *2.3
9.97419
```

(b)   *Absolute value*
       This function is represented by the sign |:

```
      |5
5
```

```
      |⁻3
3
```

(c)   *Rounding up or down*
       Numbers can be rounded up or down by means of the 'ceiling' and 'floor' functions. Thus:

```
      ⌈3.14
4
      ⌊.5+2.63
3
```

The normal operation for rounding a number up or down can thus be written:

```
      ⌈⁻.5+2.17
2
      ⌈⁻.5+2.63
3
```

When the number is already an integer, the two functions give the same result.

```
      ⌈312
312
      ⌊312
312
```

When used in their dyadic form the maximum ($\lceil$) or minimum ($\lfloor$) of two numbers can be calculated.

```
      23⌊17
17
```

1.9   The concept of variables

All the APL expressions that we have encountered so far have contained only numerical constants. However, it is possible in APL to retain a numerical value while designating a symbolic name to it, in the same way that in mathematics 'pi' or 'e' are used to denote the values 3.141592.... and 2.71828.... or 'X0' to denote a starting point in iteration, etc.

In APL the symbol ←, called the 'specification (or assignment) function', is used to create a name-value pair which we call a 'variable'.

```
      PI←3.141592
      X0←1
```

These operations result in the creation of two variables, called PI and X0 whose values are 3.141592 and 1. In an expression, these variables are referred to by their symbolic names.

```
      X0
1
```

```
      X0+2
3
```

```
      PI+X0
4.141592
```

When the APL interpreter comes across the name of a variable, it replaces it with the designated value of the variable.

```
      3×PI
9.424776
```

```
      3×3.141592
9.424776
```

It is, of course, possible to change the value of a variable, at any given moment; we say that we are assigning a new value to this variable:

```
        X0←2.5
        2×X0
5
```

The assigned value can be the result of a calculation:

```
        PI←PI+1
        PI
4.141592
```

In this example the expression PI + 1 was evaluated first, giving the result 4.141592, then this new value was assigned to PI.

The name (or *identifier*) of a variable consists of a string of letters (which may be underlined) and numbers, the first character being, of necessity, a letter. The maximum length of a name depends on the APL system used (for example 32 or 72 characters).

An error message occurs if an identifier that has not been specified is used:

```
        TOTO+3
VALUE ERROR
        TOTO+3
        ^



        TOTO
VALUE ERROR
        TOTO
        ^



        TOTO←2
        TOTO+3
5
```

'VALUE ERROR' means then, quite simply, that the computer cannot find the value associated with the name 'TOTO'.

1.10 How to use the APL system

At present, APL systems are available on a number of computers and in many different forms. There are microcomputers specially designed for APL which, like a pocket calculator, are ready to execute APL instructions as soon as they are switched on. On other machines APL is available in the form of a program called by a specific command. Finally, certain organisations offer an APL service as part of a time-sharing system, where the user identifies himself by entering in a user's sign-on number, and a password.

We shall not, however, describe the APL connection procedure since it varies dramatically from one system to another. For any given system you should refer to the manual supplied by the designer.

1.11   An example of a session

The following session took place on a T1600 computer, designed solely for APL, which operates a time-sharing system enabling several users to work simultaneously, each using his own terminal to communicate with the machine.

When a terminal is vacant it displays the following:

```
APL/16\MINES  READY
RELEASE 3.0 DECEMBER 78 T030
     ▧▧▧▧▧▧▧▧▧▧▧▧▧▧▧▧▧▧▧
```

To use APL service, you must first of all identify yourself by giving a user's *sign-on number* followed by a *password*. Theoretically, the password is known only by the person who uses the sign-on number. This procedure is called *connection* (sign-on or log-in).

To connect up, a closing bracket, followed by the sign-on number, a colon and the password must be typed in. For example:

```
)31415:SESAME
```

If the system recognises the sign-on number and the password, it gives an answer:

```
030)   83/03/21   10.08.15   SMITH
```

```
   APL/16\MINES  READY  64 K
```

Different APL systems can hide the sign-on number and password, either by not printing the characters typed in by the user, or by disguising them. This is what happened in our example.

This message gives the following information:

030)	83/03/21 10. 08. 15	SMITH
Terminal number	Date and time of connection	User's name

The APL system is now ready for use.

When you no longer require the computer's services, you must indicate this with the message:

```
      )OFF
```

sometimes followed by a colon and a new password. The system then sends back the reply:

```
030     83/03/21   10.08.35   SMI
CONNECTED    0.01.00   TO DATE    0.01.00
CPU TIME     0.00.00   TO DATE    0.00.00
```

which contains the following information:

```
      030    83/01/05  10.08.35.      SMI
```

Terminal number	Date and time of disconnection	1st 3 letters of user's name

```
      CONNECTED     0.01.00    TO DATE     0.01.00
```

Length of session in hours, minutes and seconds	Sum of the time of all the user's sessions

```
      CPU TIME    0.00.00    TO DATE    0.00.00
```

Calculation time in hours, minutes and seconds	Sum of time for all of the user's calculations

CPU stands for central processing unit.

This is what appeared on the user's terminal:

```
     APL/16\MINES   READY
RELEASE  3.0  DECEMBER  78  T030
       )▓▓▓▓▓▓▓▓▓▓▓▓▓▓▓▓▓▓▓
030)    83/03/21   10.10.08   SMITH

     APL/16\MINES   READY   64 K


        1+2+3
6
        1+4÷3
2.33333
        E←*1
        E
2.71828
        *2.3
9.97419
        ε
SYNTAX ERROR
        ε
        ∧
```

```
        E*5
148.413
        83443645÷283632
294.197
        144*.5
12
        2×3
6
        2×3×4
24
        2×3×4×5×6×7×8×9
362880
        15243*2543
LIMIT ERROR
        15243*2543
             ∧
        )OFF
030   83/03/21  10.12.49   SMI
CONNECTED   0.03.00  TO DATE   0.04.00
CPU TIME    0.00.01  TO DATE   0.00.09
```

1.12   Important points

Connection:

Disconnection:)OFF

Care with signs: $\begin{cases} \text{⁻ indicates that a constant is negative.} \\ \text{− takes the opposite of its operand (monadic).} \end{cases}$

Identifier: letter, string of letters and numbers.

Monadic functions: $+ - \times \div | \lceil | \ast$.

Dyadic functions: $+ - \times \div \lceil | \ast$.

A line is not executed until the carriage return key (CR) has been depressed.

2 HANDLING SCALARS AND VECTORS

2.1 Line correction

The computer analyses the lines in the same order as we read them, this is the principle of 'visual fidelity': the order in which the characters are typed in is irrelevant.

There is a special key on the terminal to move the carriage backwards (BS); let us look at some of the ways in which it is used:

(1) Suppose we want to calculate $(A + B) - C$, but we have already written $A + B$ before realising that the opening bracket is missing. By using the BS key we can backspace, type in the bracket, then, with the space bar (SP) complete the expression:

$(A + B) - C$

(2) If we suddenly decide to assign the result of a calculation to a variable:

$PI \times R * 2$

all we have to do is to backspace, allocate the value, then return the carriage (CR):

$C \leftarrow PI \times R * 2$

These two examples illustrate the convenience of the six free spaces at the beginning of the line.

In the same way,

$123(CR)$

is equivalent to:

$1 (SP) 3 (BS) (BS) 2 (CR)$

which displays the same result on the output device: 123.

2.2 Error correction

Sometimes, however, it is necessary to delete one or several characters that have been incorrectly entered. Instead of depressing the carriage return it is possible to backspace with the BS key as far as the error, and then to depress the 'break' key (BRK).† The system then replies by printing the character V beneath the designated position, and awaits further instructions:

```
PI←3;1415
   v
```

This operation deletes all the characters situated above and to the right of the character V.

```
PI←3;1415
   v
```

is equivalent to:

```
PI←3
```

Thus writing:

```
PI←3;1415
   v
    .141592
```

is equivalent to:

```
PI←3.141592
```

2.3   Composite characters

Certain of the APL characters such as A̲ B̲ C̲ ⊟ ⌽ ⍋ ⍒, etc., cannot be found on the keyboard. We shall not concern ourselves here with their use but with the way they are formed: these characters are obtained by superimposing two ordinary characters of the APL keyboard. This is done by striking one of the characters, backspacing and then striking the second character. Thus A̲ is formed from the letter A and the character 'underscore' (_), ⌽ from | and ○, etc. There is not necessarily a meaning for every combination of characters; for example:

```
ATY23⌿T⍳↑↓↓
CHARACTER ERROR
ATY23⊙T⍳↑↓↓
        ^
```

causes the system to print an error message and the illegal character is indicated by the following symbol: ⊙.

The principal APL characters, and in particular the composite characters, are listed in the appendix 1.

---

† On other systems CTL Z, ?, 'escape', ATTN can be used.

By way of an example, let us look at the use of the character ! (a full stop .
and an apostrophe ' superimposed). Used in its monadic form, it represents the
'factorial' function:

```
    !9
362880
```

```
      1×2×3×4×5×6×7×8×9
362880
```

If the operand X is not an integer, then !X represents the GAMMA(X+1)
function:

```
    !2.5
3.323351
```

The function applies to any number that is not a negative integer. However, the
range of application is limited by the machine. APL/1600 on a T1600 cannot
calculate !34. Certain systems, such as APL/800 on a PHILIPS P857 would
supply an answer to the following:

```
    !3210
2.765126E9860
```

2.4   APL syntax

We have already seen that some expressions do not have any meaning
for the APL system, such as '1+'.

Indeed, to be understood by the interpreter every APL phrase must obey
APL syntax in the same way that phrases of the English language obey English
syntax. Just as the phrase 'apples they are' does not obey English syntax so the
phrase 1+ does not obey APL syntax.

Fortunately, however, it can be said that APL syntax is defined by a small
number of simple rules, compared to the number that govern English, or even
certain other programming languages. There is no exception to any rule. An APL
expression may consist of a single operand, a monadic function followed by an
operand, or a dyadic function applied to two operands. This definition can be
expressed in the following way (where the vertical line indicates the possible
alternatives):

⟨*expression*⟩ = ⟨*operand*⟩|
    ⟨*monadic function*⟩ ⟨*right operand*⟩|
    ⟨*operand*⟩ ⟨*dyadic function*⟩ ⟨*right operand*⟩

An operand may be a constant, a variable, or an expression, sometimes within parentheses:

$$\langle operand \rangle = \langle constant \rangle \, | \langle variable \rangle | \, (\langle expression \rangle)$$
$$\langle right \ operand \rangle = \langle expression \rangle$$

However, when the left operand obeys the description ⟨*operand*⟩, the right operand is in fact the expression situated to the right of the function. Applying these grammatical rules to the following example:

    1+2÷3-4

We have:

$$\langle expression \rangle = \langle operand \rangle \ \langle dyadic \ function \rangle \ \langle right \ operand \rangle$$

where

$$\langle operand \rangle = \langle constant \rangle = 1$$
$$\langle dyadic \ function \rangle = +$$
$$\langle right \ operand \rangle = \langle expression \ 1 \rangle$$

which gives

$$\langle expression \rangle = 1 + \langle expression \ 1 \rangle$$

and, following the same pattern, we obtain:

$$\langle expression \ 1 \rangle = 2 \div \langle expression \ 2 \rangle$$
$$\langle expression \ 2 \rangle = 3 - \langle expression \ 3 \rangle$$
$$\langle expression \ 3 \rangle = 4$$

We can deduce, therefore, that the ⟨*expression*⟩ is calculated *from right to left without any of the functions taking precedence.* Thus the subtraction takes place before the division simply because this function is situated further to the right in the expression. The above example could be written using the standard convention:

    1+(2÷(3-(4)))

The calculation is carried out in the following manner:

$$\langle expression \ 3 \rangle = 4$$
$$\langle expression \ 2 \rangle = 3 - 4 = {}^{-}1$$
$$\langle expression \ 1 \rangle = 2 \div {}^{-}1 = {}^{-}2$$
$$\langle expression \rangle = 1 + {}^{-}2 = {}^{-}1$$

Let us try typing in the following:

    1+2÷3-4
 ⁻1

but:

```
      1-4+2÷3
¯3.66667
```

Let us not take another expression, this time using parentheses:

```
      (1+2×3)÷3
2.33333
```

In order to carry out the division the computer first of all evaluates the operands, then the expression inside the brackets. We can see how, in this particular instance, using the brackets meant that the task 1 + 2 x 3 had to be executed before the division by 3.

The following rules should thus be remembered:

> No function takes precedence during execution;
> The execution takes place from right to left;
> The order in which an instruction is obeyed can be modified by using brackets.

For example:

```
      2×3+4
14
```

```
      (2×3)+4
10
```

It should be pointed out, however, that just because an expression obeys APL syntax does not necessarily mean that it can be evaluated; no more than a phrase obeying English syntax necessarily has any meaning. As an illustration one could compare the expressons '1 ÷ 0' and 'the chairs drink buttermilk'†.

2.5   Control language

Some expressions are accepted by the computer even though they do not obey APL syntax. Thus:

```
      )OFF
```

which we have already met, is an example of such an expression. These expressions, known as 'system commands' trigger certain actions which are not calculations, such as connection and disconnection. These commands take the following

---

† Such a phrase might possibly stand a chance of being accepted by a literary panel but would probably be rejected by a scientific board of examiners.

form:

>)⟨*symbolic name*⟩{⟨*complements*⟩}†

There is also a very useful command with which the names of the defined variables can be identified during a work session. This command is written

)*VARS*
PI

Here, the system replies by showing that a defined variable exists, called PI. Let us invent some others:

        A←1
        B←A+1
)*VARS*
A   *B*   *PI*
        C←A×B
)*VARS*
A   *B*   *C*   *PI*

These variables are displayed in alphabetical order.

Yet another command enables all the defined variables to be retained for subsequent use. This is written:

)*SAVE SESSION*
83/03/21 10.21.11 SESSION

The set of variables constitutes a 'workspace' or **WS** which is saved under the name SESSION. A message indicates the date and time of operation and repeats the name with which it is possible, at any moment during the present or any subsequent session, to recover the workspace in the state in which it was saved. This is done by using the command)LOAD.

)*LOAD SESSION*
SAVED   83/03/21   10.21.11

The message indicates the date and time when the workspace was last saved.

)*VARS*
A   *B*   *C*   *PI*

We have now recovered the variable names; let us ask for the values of some of them:

        B
2
        PI
3.14159

† The braces indicate that the complements depend on the command. See appendix 2.

A variable in the workspace can be deleted using the command)ERASE followed by the name of the variable (or possibly by several names separated by spaces). For example:

```
      )ERASE A B
      )VARS
C        PI
```

2.6   Logical type

Comparing two pieces of data is a standard problem in all programming languages. For this, APL has the comparison functions:

$$< \leqslant = \neq \geqslant >$$

whose meanings are obvious. For an expression such as $A \leqslant B$ the reply is 'true' if A is less than or equal to B and 'false' if it is greater. In APL 'true' and 'false' are denoted by 1 and 0 respectively:

```
      3<5
1
```

```
      4≠4
0
```

```
      5≥9
0
```

The values obtained by such comparisons are said to be of the logical type. In APL, this type is a subset of the numeric mode. Consider the following example:

```
      A←4
      B←2
```

```
      D←6
      C←4
```

The solution of the problem: 'How many of the three following conditions are true?'

```
      A≥B      A≠C      B<D
```

can be written:

```
      (A≥B)+(A≠C)+B<D
2
```

The result is an integer between 0 and 3 depending on the number of relations verified.

Elements of the logical type can be handled using other functions. Note in particular the $\wedge$ (and) and $\vee$ (or) function:

      0 $\wedge$ 0
0
      0 $\wedge$ 1
0
      1 $\wedge$ 0
0
      1 $\wedge$ 1
1

      0 $\vee$ 0
0
      0 $\vee$ 1
1
      1 $\vee$ 0
1
      1 $\vee$ 1
1

For example, to find out if the three conditions stated in the preceding problem are simultaneously true, we would write:

$$(A \geq B) \wedge (A \neq C) \wedge B < D$$
0

Similarly we might be interested in finding out whether at least one of the propositions was true. Using the '$\vee$' function we would write:

$$(A \geq B) \vee (A \neq C) \vee B < D$$
1

2.7   Character type

In APL, it is possible to manipulate data of the character type, just as with data of the numerical type. A character constant is denoted by a character placed within quotes:

    'A'   '4'   'ϕ'   '+'   '▤'

The value of the character type is displayed by the computer as a single character, with the quotes removed:

    'X'
X
    '6'
6

```
      A←'3'
      A
3
      ''''
'
```

It is important to note that for a character constant 'quote' must appear twice to produce one single quote.

Obviously it is impossible to carry out arithmetic operations on elements of the character type:

```
      'S'+3
DOMAIN ERROR
      'S'+3
      ∧
```

```
      A+2
DOMAIN ERROR
      A+2
      ∧
```

The perceptive reader will have already worked out why this last expression is incorrect. However the comparison functions = and ≠ (and only these) are valid for characters:

```
      'A'≠'C'
1
```

```
      'Z'='ρ'
0
```

We shall see later how these characters operate, and more generally, the uses of the non-numerical aspects of data processing.

2.8 Dealing with sets

So far we have only considered handling simple elements (called scalars). Does this mean to say that APL is incapable of dealing with sets of more than one element, such as vectors or matrices? Fortunately this is certainly not the case – indeed, we shall discover later that APL is a very useful tool for this type of operation.

A numerical vector is represented by a series of numbers separated from each other by one or more spaces. Likewise, the computer prints vector results in this form:

```
      1  2  3
1     2  3
```

Everything that has been said so far about scalars can be applied to vectors (element by element):

```
      1  2  3+2  3  5
3     5  8
      1  5÷2  3
.5    1.66667
      1  2  3  4×4  3  2  1
4     6  6  4
```

```
      A←1  3  5  8
      B←1.5  2  3  5.6  8  11.2
      A+B
LENGTH ERROR
      A+B
      ^
```

In the second example it is impossible for the computer to add the two vectors (element by element) since they are not the same length.

By using the new function ρ (rho) in its monadic form, the dimensions of an object can be discovered:

```
      ρ2  3  5  5
4
```
_____ *Dimensions of the vector* 2 3 5 5 (*number of elements*)

It is thus possible to determine the dimensions of A and B:

```
      ρA
4
```

```
      ρB
6
```

and even to know directly if it is possible for the two operands to be added:

```
      (ρA)=ρB
0
```

Notice that if we had written $\rho A = \rho B$, we would have compared A to ρB, then applied the operator ρ to the result of the comparison.

If the object is a scalar it is said to be 'dimensionless' and the result of the application of ρ to this scalar is thus void:

```
ρ'A'          ⎫
              ⎬ void results
ρ3            ⎭
```

Note that the result of applying ρ to an object is always a vector. If the object in question is a scalar, the result is the 'empty vector'.

```
        ρρ2  3  5  5                    Result of ρ applied to the vector of
1 ◄─────────────────────────────────── dimension 2 3 5 5
```

```
        ρρ3                            Result of ρ applied to the (empty)
0 ◄─────────────────────────────────── vector of dimension 3
```

The result of this double application of the function is called the rank (the dimension of the object). A scalar is thus an object of rank 0, a vector an object of rank 1. We shall see later how this idea can be generalised to include arrays.

If in an arithmetic operation or a logical comparison one of the two operands is a scalar and the other a vector, the scalar is *extended to the dimensions of the other operand*:

```
        3   4   5   5+2
5   6   7   7
```

```
        'A'='CDARA4'
0   0   1   0   1   0
```

A character vector is a series of characters between quotes; these vectors are sometimes called 'character strings'.

```
        'ABDε12QW'
ABDε12QW
```

```
        ρ'CAT'
3
```

Quotes must be doubled up:

```
        '6''Tε''''o*'''
6'Tε''o*'
```

The following are operations on character vectors:

```
        'E'='THE CAT' ◄─────────────────────────── The scalar is extended
0   0   1   0   0   0   0
        'THE CHICK'='THE   CAT '
1   1   1   1   0   0   0   0   0
```

2.9   Reduction

We are now going to look at one of the most useful operators in APL: reduction. This operator, represented by the character /, modifies the way in which a function is applied to data. For example, suppose:

```
V←2  3  5  8  6
```

The reduction of the vector V by the function + is written:

```
+/V
```

The operation consists of applying the function + between all the elements of the vector V.

```
      (+/V)
24
```

is equivalent to

```
      2+3+5+8+6
24
```

The operation ×/V calculates the product of the elements of V; it is in effect equivalent to:

```
      ×/V
1440
```

```
      2×3×5×8×6
1440
```

The operation −/V is no less interesting: it calculates the alternating sum of the elements of the vector V. In fact, it is equivalent to

```
      -/V
2
```

```
      2-3-5-8-6
2
```

Since the order of evaluation is from right to left, this expression is equivalent to:

```
      (2+5+6)-3+8
2
```

The same phenomenon occurs for the expression which calculates the alternating product of the elements of V:

```
      ÷/V
2.5
```

```
      2÷3÷5÷8÷6
2.5
      (2×5×6)÷3×8
2.5
```

For a logical vector the functions ∧ and ∨ can be applied:

```
      X←1 1 1 0 1 0
      ∧/X
0
```

```
      ∨/X
1
```

Here are some examples of the ways in which some of the functions can be used.

The mean of the vector elements:

```
      (+/V)÷ρV
4.8
```
We could also write +/V÷ρV but this involves a greater number of divisions

The geometric mean:

```
      (×/V)*÷ρV
4.28225
```

The number of Ts in a phrase:

```
      +/'T'='THE CAT SAT ON THE MAT'
5
```

An approximation for e:

```
      +/÷!0 1 2 3 4 5 6 7 8 9 10
2.71828
```

In this example we have used the sum of the inverse of the factorials of the integers from 0 to N, with N equal to 10 here. Now a special function exists which generates the list of the first N integers. This is the monadic function 'iota':

```
      ι5
1 2 3 4 5
      ι13
1 2 3 4 5 6 7 8 9 10 11 12 13
```

The calculation of e thus becomes:

```
     1++/÷!ι30
2.71828
```

Notice that the precision of the calculation is the same as it was with ten elements.

2.10   Important points

In APL the principle of visual fidelity is used.

Error correction: special key.

Evaluation of expressions: strictly right to left with no functions having precedence.

System commands:
)VARS
)ERASE
)SAVE
)LOAD

Monadic functions: $! \rho \iota .$

Dyadic functions: $< \leqslant = \neq \geqslant > \wedge \vee$

Monadic operator: $/$

3   DEFINING AND USING A FUNCTION

3.1   User functions

Suppose we wanted to calculate the hypotenuse of a right-angled triangle; in APL, we could write:

```
A←3
B←4
((A*2)+B*2)*.5
```
5

If we wanted to calculate the hypotenuses of several different triangles, we would be forced to rewrite these three lines each time. The method appears to be all the more cumbersome when the final result can only be obtained after a great number of expressions have been evaluated (as in the calculation of the eigenvalues of a matrix, for example).

It would thus be useful to be able to define (once and once only) this set of instructions; this is called an algorithm. Each time it is required we simply have to call it and ask for it to be executed. In order to call it, however, we must give it a name. Thus we are going to define a new type of APL object. We already know how to define name–value pairs (variables). Now we want to construct name–algorithm pairs which are called *user functions*.

3.2   Defining a function

So far, every instruction typed in at the terminal was carried out immediately on pressing carriage return. The APL machine has been functioning like a sophisticated calculator in *execution mode*. However, the expressions that we are going to enter to create our user function will not be carried out immediately. It is therefore necessary to change the role of the interpreter by switching to *definition mode*. For this we use the character 'del' (∇). This character is followed by the name (or identifier) which is assigned to the function. It must obey the same rules as a variable identifier (see 1.9). For example:

```
∇HYP
[1]
```

means that we are in definition mode and that the function is called HYP. When this line is received by the interpreter, the latter replies with the number 1 in square brackets indicating that it is ready to receive the first expression of the algorithm. Let us write this expression:

```
[1]    ((A*2)+B*2)*.5
[2]
```

The system waits for the second line of the function. But the definition of our algorithm is complete. Therefore we must change from definition mode to execution mode. This is indicated by the same character 'del':

```
[2]    ∇
```

The interpreter will now execute all the expressions that we send to it, including the function that has just been created. To call it, we simply type in its name:

```
      HYP
5
```

Let us give A and B some other values:

```
      A←11
      B←18
      HYP
21.095
```

If we now decide that we want to print out the length of the sides A and B as well as the hypotenuse, the algorithm of the function must be modified. We must move once again into definition mode and indicate the name of the function to be completed:

```
      ∇HYP
[2]
```

The system replies with [2] since line 1 already exists. Now we can add new expressions (also called *instructions*) to the function, after which we return to execution mode:

```
[2]    A
[3]    B
[4]    ∇
```

Execution of the function gives:

```
      HYP
21.095
11
18
```

3.3 Correcting a function

Often the result of calculations carried out by a function is needed within expressions. In our example the result of HYP might be used to determine the perimeter of the triangle. This presupposes that the result of the function can be assigned to a variable and reused in the perimeter formula. Let us try:

```
        C←HYP
21.095
11
18
SYNTAX  ERROR
        C←HYP
        ∧
```

An error message appears. In fact, we are not able to assign the result of our function outside the function. Later we shall give an elegant solution to this problem, but for the time being we shall be content with a simple solution which consists of assigning the result of the hypotenuse calculation to a variable within the algorithm. To do this we must modify line 1. First, we move to definition mode. The system asks for the fourth instruction in the algorithm. Now, we do not wish to add lines, but to modify an existing one. We indicate this by giving the number of the line to be corrected and the position in the line. These two numbers are separated by the character 'quad' (□) and placed between square brackets.

```
        ∇HYP
[4]     [1□10]
```
_____ *Position in the line*
_____ *Number of the line to be modified*

The system prints the line corresponding to the number given, places the carriage beneath the 11th character in this line and awaits a correction instruction. Only the following characters can be used for this instruction:

   (1) either a slash (/) which is a request to cancel the character immediately above it;

   (2) or a number between 1 and 9 which is a request to insert the corresponding number of spaces to the left of the character situated immediately above the number.

An error message will appear if any other character is used in a modification instruction. The carriage is positioned beneath the characters to be corrected by using the BS and SP keys.

```
[1]     ((A*2)+B*2)*.5
        //5
```

The two opening brackets will be deleted and five spaces inserted before A. The system prints the line with the changes made. It is then possible to complete the line and to return to execution mode.

```
[1]      C←((  A*2)+B*2)*.5
[2]      ∇
```

The observant reader will without doubt have noticed that it was not strictly necessary to delete the brackets. One could quite simply have written:

```
[1]      ((A*2)+B*2)*.5
         2
[1]      C←((A*2)+B*2)*.5 ∇
```

Note in passing that the request for return to execution mode could have been made on the same line. The principle of visual fidelity still applies.

Finally, let us look at the system's response when a modification command contains illegal characters:

```
[1]      ((A*2)+B*2)*.5
            +
EDITING ERROR
[2]
```

An error message appears; line 1 has not been modified. We just need to give the modification instruction again:

```
[2]      [1□10]
```

etc.

Let us try executing the function:

```
         HYP
11
18


         C
21.095
         A+B+C
50.095
```

3.4   The function heading

We have found a method of calculating the perimeter of the triangle. However, the function HYP is not very satisfactory in its present form. Indeed, before calculating the length of a new hypotenuse, we have to specify the relevant values of A and B which necessitates writing two lines. The function would be far more convenient if specifying the values were simpler. There is a way of doing this.

The language functions that we have encountered so far ($+, \times, \div, \ldots$) have had one or two operands. At the moment the HYP function does not have one at all. It is said to be *niladic*. But it can be rendered either monadic or dyadic depending on what the user needs. One simply indicates the name of the operand or operands in the function heading (which at the moment only contains its name).

Let us return to our example. Obviously HYP has two operands which are the length of the sides. Let us correct the function heading to make it dyadic:

```
      ∇HYP
[4]    [0□7]◄─────────── Request for heading modification
[0]    HYP
       9
[0]    A          HYP    B∇
```

Any request for execution of HYP must now specify the values of the operands. These can be constants or defined variables, or, more generally, expressions:

```
      A HYP B
11
18
      C
21.095
      10 HYP 15
10
15


      C
18.0278
      (4*2) HYP B-A
16
7
      C
17.4642
```

The names of the variables A and B used in the function heading are only there to enable the interpreter to recognise the operands inside the function called with HYP. Thus, every time the name of the variable A appears (inside the function), it represents the value of the left operand of the function called, while B represents the value of the right operand. A and B are called *formal parameters*, or *dummy variables*, and the values assigned to them at the time of calling, the *effective* or *real parameters*.

There is one more modification we need to make so that the use of the function is the same as that of any of the language functions. We were able to use the result of the calculation by the method of assigning it to a variable C inside the function. This variable can appear later in other expressions. It would be very convenient to be able to use the result directly without recourse to the intermediate variable C. To this end we indicate in the function heading that the function yields a result with a given name, as we did for the operands. We must not forget to specify a result for this name in the function's algorithm. We shall choose C as the name of the result since the value of the hypotenuse is assigned to this name in line 1. Let us modify the function:

```
      ∇HYP
[4]      [□]◄──────────────── Request for the function to be printed
   ∇ A HYP B
[1]    C←((A*2)+B*2)*.5
[2]    A
[3]    B
   ∇
[4]    [0□1]
[0]    A HYP B
       2
[0]    C←A HYP B
[1]    ∇
```

Execution of the function gives:

```
      10 HYP 15
10
15
18.0278
```

The result of the calculation is printed. This result can be assigned to a variable in the instruction for execution:

```
      D←10 HYP 15
10
15
```

The value of the hypotenuse no longer appears since this has been specified. It is contained in the variable D:

```
      D
18.0278
```

The result can be used directly in calculating the perimeter:

```
      10+15+10 HYP 15
10
15
43.0278
```

The printing of the length of the sides A and B is now rather a nuisance. To delete it we must remove lines 2 and 3 of the function. The command used to

delete a line numbered i is [i↓]. More generally, the command [i j↓] deletes
lines i to j inclusive.

```
      ∇HYP
[4]     [2  3↓]
[4]     [□]
     ∇ C←A HYP B
[1]     C←((A*2)+B*2)*.5
     ∇
[4]     ∇
```

Notice that the system is still requesting line 4. It is only on returning to
execution mode that it reorganises the numbering of the lines.

```
      ∇HYP
[2]     [□]
     ∇ C←A HYP  B
[1]     C←((A*2)+B*2)*.5
     ∇
[2]     ∇
```

The instruction for printing which we have used above could have been
written in one line:

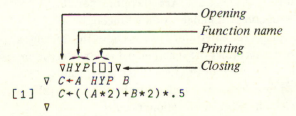

```
∇HYP[□]∇ ←——————— Closing
     ∇ C←A HYP  B
[1]     C←((A*2)+B*2)*.5
     ∇
```

In this latter form, the function is used in the same way as any dyadic function
of the language. One can thus consider it as a valid addition to the set of
primitive functions available to the user.

```
      A←6                          3+4
      B←7                 7
      3 HYP  4                     A+B
5                        13
      A HYP  B                     Q←A+5×2
9.21955                           Q
      P←A HYP  5×2        16
      3+4+3 HYP  4                 3×4×3+4
12                       84
```

3.5   System commands

In the same way that one can find all the defined variables in a workspace with the command)VARS, the command)FNS gives the names of the
functions.

```
        )VARS
A       B       C       D       P       PI      Q


        )FNS
HYP
```

What happens when the system detects an error in a function? Let us define the function $F(X) = X^2 + 1/X$.

```
        ∇R←F  X
[1]     R←(X*2)+÷X
[2]     ∇
```

Now let us ask for execution with different values of X:

```
        F  3
9.33333
        F  5
25.2
        F  0
DOMAIN  ERROR
F[1]    R←(X*2)+÷X
                ∧
```

For $X = 0$, $F(X)$ is not definable since $1/X$ is not. APL therefore indicates a domain error for the inverse function ($\div$) in line 1 of the function.

Execution of the function F has been interrupted as a result of the domain error. We shall see later that one can correct the function and resume execution within the interrupted function. To allow for this facility the system stores information on the interrupted functions, retrievable with the command)SI (state interrupt) which indicates where the interruptions occurred:

```
        )SI
F[1]      *
```

In this case,)SI shows that we were interrupted on line 1 of the function F. If we introduce another error:

```
        C←'A' HYP 3
DOMAIN  ERROR
HYP[1]  C←((A*2)+B*2)*.5
                ∧
        )SI
HYP[1]    *
F[1]      *
```

Two interruptions are now stored. This information takes up space and consequently we need to be able to delete it from time to time. To do this we just type in a right arrow '→' which allows an exit from the most recently interrupted function. Here, two arrows are needed:

```
        →
        )SI
F[1]        *
        →
        )SI
        →
DEPTH  ERROR  ←──────────────  The error message indicates that there are
        →                      no longer any interrupted functions
        ∧
```

With the instruction)SIC (state interrupt clear), the interruption statements can be cleared in one operation.

3.6   Branching

It will have been noticed that the lines of a function are executed in ascending order. When we call a function, the APL system begins with execution of line 1, then 2, etc, up to the last line. This prohibits the use of complex calculations that involve either repeating execution of a line until a certain condition has been satisfied, or using one formula rather than another depending on the value of an expression. For example, to solve a quadratic equation $AX^2 + BX + C = 0$, we have three cases:

(1)   if the discriminant is zero: a double root $-B/2A$;

(2)   if the discriminant is positive: two real roots:

$$(-B \pm (B^2 - 4AC)^{1/2})/2A;$$

(3)   if the discriminant is negative: two complex roots:

$$(-B \pm i(-(B^2 - 4AC))^{1/2})/2A.$$

We are now going to introduce a function that allows us to indicate explicitly the number of the line to be executed: this is the *branching* function symbolised by the right arrow: →.

This function only exists in the monadic form. To go to line 5 of a function, we write:

→5

If we indicate a line number that does not exist in the definition of the function, execution of the function is terminated. In particular a branching to line 0 (which is impossible to execute) always terminates execution.

Branching is a function like any other and its operand can be any APL expression whose result gives a line number.

→7+X=0

can be translated as go to line 8 if X = 0 and line 7 if not.

```
      →?10
```

means go to any line at random between 1 and 10.

The monadic function ? (random selection) is applied to a positive integer value and returns an integer (chosen randomly) between 1 and the given value.

Let us try writing a function F(X) giving X if X is greater than 0, and 0 if not.

```
        ∇Y←F X
[1]     →2+2×X>0
[2]     Y←0
[3]     →0
[4]     Y+X∇
```

$2 \times X > 0$ equals 0 if X is negative or zero and 2 if not. Line 1 is thus equivalent to going to 2 if $X \leqslant 0$ and 4 if not.

Notice that we terminate the definition of the function at the end of line 4 with the character ∇. In fact, this example can be dealt with in a much simpler fashion by using the function 'maximum':

```
        ∇Y←F X
[1]     Y←0⌈X∇
```

This is essentially of academic interest.

The right operand of → could be a vector, in which case the branching takes place on the line corresponding to the first element of the vector. If the vector is empty, execution continues in sequence. We could then write:

```
        ∇Y←F X
[1]     →0×ι0≥Y←X
[2]     Y←0∇
```

> *In fact if* $X \leqslant 0$ *then* $0 \geqslant Y \leftarrow X$ *equals* 1 *and* $0 \times \iota 1$ *equals* 0,
> *if* $X > 0$ *then* $0 \geqslant Y \leftarrow X$ *equals* 0 *and* $0 \times \iota 0$ *is the empty vector.*

Gradually, as we come across new functions, we shall be able to construct new forms of branching.

Let us return to the preceding form, which is used very frequently and can be formalised.

> → N × ι ⟨*condition*⟩

enables us to go to line N if the condition is true (N × ι1 equals N) or to continue in sequence if it is false (N × ι0 gives an empty vector)

> → N × ι ⟨*condition*⟩ is equivalent to *go to N if* ⟨*condition*⟩ is true

Let us try writing the function that resolves a quadratic equation. We shall begin by calculating the discriminant:

```
      ∇ RESOLVE
[1]     D←(B×B)-4×A×C
```

Now we want to be able to branch to the appropriate procedure for D = 0, but we do not know on which line this procedure begins. We shall identify this line with a variable called a *label* which will take the value of the number of the line in which it appears followed by the character ':'. We therefore write:

```
[2]    →DOUBLE×ι0=D
[3]    →COMPLEX×ι0>D
```

Then dealing with the case of real roots:

```
[4]    'REAL ROOTS'
[5]    ((-B)+D*.5)÷2×A
[6]    ((-B)-D*.5)÷2×A
[7]    →0
```

Now let us deal with the case of complex roots beginning the line with 'COMPLEX:'

```
[8]  COMPLEX:'COMPLEX ROOTS'
[9]    'REAL PART'
[10]   -B÷2×A
[11]   'IMAGINARY PART'
[12]   ((-D)*.5)÷2×A
[13]   →0
[14] DOUBLE:'DOUBLE ROOT'
[15]   -B÷2×A
       ∇
```

The label COMPLEX is thus equal to 8 and DOUBLE is 14. This way we have avoided calculating the number of lines of the function before writing it. Furthermore, if we modify it by deleting or adding lines, we do not have to correct the branchings; APL is responsible for assigning the correct values to COMPLEX and DOUBLE. Finally, a judicious choice of label names will make the algorithm easier to understand.

 Let us test the function:

```
        A←1
        B←2
        C←1
        RESOLVE
DOUBLE ROOT
‾1
        A←1
        B←1
        C←1
        RESOLVE
COMPLEX ROOTS
REAL PART
‾.5
IMAGINARY PART
.866025
        B←4
        RESOLVE
REAL ROOTS
‾.267949
‾3.73205
```

Another area where branching is indispensable is in iterative calculation. Suppose we want to write a function calculating a square root using a sequence:

$$\mu_n = \frac{1}{2}\left(\mu_{n-1} + \frac{A}{\mu_{n-1}}\right).$$

We can write:

```
     ∇  R←SQRT A
[1]     R←1
[2]     I←(R+A÷R)÷2
[3]     →0×ιEPS>|R-I
[4]     R←I
[5]     →2
     ∇
        EPS←÷10000
```

EPS will stop the calculation according to the precision required.

3.7   Trace

Since we cannot be sure of the progression through the algorithm we would like to be able to check its execution step by step. APL provides a special function which prints the results of calculations carried out in certain specified lines of the function. The *trace* function belongs to the category *system functions* and is called □ST (set trace, or in APL systems with a slightly different syntax □TRACE)

```
        2 3 □ST 'SQRT' ←————————Function name
  2  3           └————————————————Number of lines to be traced
```

During execution of SQRT, each time the system meets one of the lines to be traced it indicates the name of the function, the number of the line and the result of the calculation carried out on that line. If the operation to be traced is a branch, the number of the line to which control is passed is preceded by an arrow.

```
        SQRT 30
SQRT[2] 15.5
SQRT[3]→
        SQRT[2] 8.71774
SQRT[3]→
SQRT[2] 6.0795
SQRT[3]→
SQRT[2] 5.50706
SQRT[3]→
SQRT[2] 5.47731
SQRT[3]→
SQRT[2] 5.47723
SQRT[3]→0
5.47731
```

The algorithm is correct, but the result supplied is not the best approximation. The function must therefore be modified:

```
        ∇SQRT[1☐10]
[1]     R←1
         /1
[1]     R←I
[2]     [0.5]I←1
[0.6]   [2☐10]
[2]     I←(R+A÷R)÷2
         /1 /1   /1
[2]     R←(I+A÷I)÷2
```

We make a request to modify line 1 and then we make the correction. We then add a line above line 1, giving it a decimal number less than 1 with no more than two decimal places, and we type in the expression to be inserted: [0.5] I←1. The system then asks for the next line and we reply with a request for a correction to line 2. What does the function look like now?

```
[3]     [☐]
     ∇ R←SQRT  A
[0.5] I←1
[1]     R←I
[2]     R←(I+A÷I)÷2
[3]     →0×ιEPS>|R-I
[4]     R←I
[5]     →2
     ∇
```

Finally, line 1 must be deleted (since it duplicates line 4) and line 4 must be modified:

```
[6]     [1↓]
[6]     [4]I←R∇
```

What does it give on execution?

```
        SQRT 30
SQRT[2] 15.5
SQRT[3]→
        SQRT[2] 8.71774
SQRT[3]→
SQRT[2] 6.0795
SQRT[3]→
SQRT[2] 5.50706
SQRT[3]→
SQRT[2] 5.47731
SQRT[3]→
SQRT[2] 5.47723
SQRT[3]→0
5.47723
```

The result is more satisfactory. We can now cancel the trace with another system function □RT (reset trace, or □TRACE):

```
      2 3 □RT 'SQRT'
2   3
      SQRT 4
2
      SQRT 17
4.12311
```

The two preceding system functions can be used in monadic form. In this form they enable one to trace or cancel the trace of any line in the function.

3.8   Interruption of execution

We can also ask the system to stop at certain lines before executing them. The corresponding system function is □SS (set stop, or □STOP in other APL systems):

```
      3 □SS 'SQRT'
3
```

Before executing line 3, the system prints the name of the function followed by the line number and a star:

```
      SQRT 25
SQRT[3] *
```

Now we can ask for the values of R and I:

```
      I
1
```

```
      R
13
```

The command)SI indicates that we have been interrupted at line 3 as in the case of an error:

```
      )SI
SQRT[3] *
```

Let us restart execution:

```
      →3
SQRT[3] *
```

Once again we stop at line 3:

```
        I
13
        R
7.46154
       →3
SQRT[3] *
        I
7.46154
        R
5.40603
```

To resume execution we can also write →ι0, an expression that results in a branching at the interrupted line (its number is of importance):

```
       →ι0
SQRT[3] *
        I
5.40603
        R
5.01525
       )SI
SQRT[3] *
       →3
SQRT[3] *
       →3
SQRT[3] *
       →3
5
```

To cancel the stop control, we use the system function □RS (reset stop, or □STOP):

```
    3 □RS 'SQRT'
3
```

Like the preceding functions these can be used in monadic form. Let us test the function by giving EPS the value 0:

```
    EPS←0
    SQRT 4
```

The system does not reply! The function is doubtless in an infinite loop. Let us interrupt the execution by using the interrupt key:

```
    SQRT[3] *
```

The execution has been stopped on line 3. Let us look for the error:

```
        R
    2
        I
    2
```

The test is therefore incorrect since it stops the iteration when the absolute value of $R - I$ is less than EPS, in this case negative. Let us correct it:

```
        ∇SQRT[3□10]
[3]     →0×ιEPS>|R-I
                /1
[3]     →0×ιEPS≥|R-I
[4]     ∇
        SQRT 4
2
        SQRT 30
5.47723
```

Having used the system for a time, we have accumulated a certain number of variables and functions in our workspace:

```
        )FNS
F         RESOLVE SQRT
        )VARS
A         B         C         D         EPS       I         R
```

Instead of destroying all these objects with the command)ERASE, we can reinitialise our workspace by simply typing in:

```
        )CLEAR
CLEAR WS
```

The system destroys all existing objects (variables, functions, interruption vectors):

```
        )FNS
        )VARS
        )SI
```

3.9   Important points

Two modes of functioning:

execution (or normal),
definition.

Function definition:

Arguments	Without result	With result
0 → niladic	∇ FUNC	∇ R ← FUNC
1 → monadic	∇ FUNC B	∇ R ← FUNC B
2 → dyadic	∇ A FUNC B	∇ R ← A FUNC B

Function correction:

[n]	position at line n;
[n □ p]	editing of line n;
[□]	printing;
[n↓]	deletion of line n;
[n p↓]	deletion of lines n to p inclusive;

Label.

Function →

)FNS)SI)SIC)CLEAR.

Debugging, interruption:

□ST, □RT, □SS, □RS.

4.1   The array

So far, we have learnt how to deal with simple objects, which are constants (numerical, logical and character) and we have seen that a collection of constants of the same type can be structured to form compound objects: vectors. There are compound structures in addition to these which are frequently used, for example matrices. For a language to be easy to use, it must be possible to organise data into a form that is suited to its needs. It is thus essential to be able to use more general objects than vectors. These objects are called *arrays*.

4.2   Definition

Generally speaking an array is defined:

by the set of constants of which it is composed;
by its structure.

The structure is given by the dimensions of the array. Thus, to construct a vector, the number of elements must be specified, and to generate a matrix the number of lines and columns must be given.

To structure a set of data in APL we use the dyadic function 'rho' (ρ). As its right operand it has the set of constituent values, and the dimensions as the left.

```
      M←2 3ρι6
      M
1    2    3
4    5    6
      2 3ρι6
1    2    3
4    5    6
      T←2 3 4ρι20
      T
1    2    3    4
5    6    7    8
9    10   11   12

13   14   15   16
17   18   19   20
1    2    3    4
```

The array is filled by taking the elements in the order in which they occur in the right operand. If the number of elements in the latter is not large enough to fill the whole structure, it is completed cyclically. The first dimension is the number of rows, the second the number of columns. Specification is carried out by varying the indices from right to left.

Suppose T(i,j,k) is the current element of an array of dimensions n,m,p; the order of specification is as follows:

$$T(1,1,1), T(1,1,2), \ldots T(1,1,p), T(1,2,1), \ldots T(1,2,p), \ldots, T(n,m,p)$$

In other words, the array is filled line by line. The right hand argument can take any form.

```
        V←6ρM
        V
1    2    3    4    5    6
```

```
        3 8ρT
1     2     3     4     5     6     7     8
9    10    11    12    13    14    15    16
17   18    19    20     1     2     3     4
```

The monadic function ρ applied to a structure gives its dimensions. Thus:

```
        ρV
6
        ρM
2    3
```

```
        ρT
2    3    4
```

The result is a vector to which we can apply the function ρ. We thus obtain the number of dimensions, in other words, the rank of the structure:

```
        ρρV
1
        ρρM
2
```

```
        ρρT
3
```

Finally, if C is a scalar, then it is dimensionless and its rank is equal to 0.

```
        ρC←?100
                    ←——————— Empty vector
        ρρC
0
```

4.3   Operating on arrays

Since an array is characterised by its content and structure, the functions applied to it must consequently change either one or other or both of these. We can thus identify three types of function:

scalar functions,
restructuring functions,
mixed functions.

(a)   Scalar functions

These change the content without altering the structure. All the monadic and dyadic scalar functions which we have seen in relation to constants and vectors also apply to arrays; this simplifies considerably the writing of operations. Let us take two matrices M1 and M2, of equal dimensions; the operation whose result gives the matrix M such that:

$$M_{ij} = M1_{ij} + M2_{ij} \ \forall \ i,j$$

is simply written:

$$M \leftarrow M1 + M2$$

When the function is dyadic, the two operands should be identical in structure. However, if one of them is a scalar, it is automatically extended to the dimensions of the other.

```
      M←2 3ρ¯2 6 ¯4 3 0 5                      (×M)×|M
      M                              ¯2   6      ¯4
¯2   6    ¯4                          3   0       5
 3   0     5                               M÷2
      ×M                             ¯1   3      ¯2
¯1   1    ¯1                         1.5   0     2.5
 1   0     1                               2÷M
      |M                            DOMAIN  ERROR
 2   6    4                                2÷M
 3   0    5                                 ∧
```

The error message occurs because we have left the domain for which the function is valid (division by 0).

```
      M+6  8  7
RANK  ERROR
      M+6  8  7
      ∧
```

Here we see a new type of error: the ranks of the operands are incompatible.

In addition to the scalar functions we have already met, there is one that is specifically for operation on square matrices: inversion. This is the monadic (domino) function ⊞ (derived from □ and ÷).

```
      M←?3 3ρ5
      M
5   3   2
3   4   4
5   2   5


      ⊞M
.2553191      ‾.2340426      8.51064E‾2
.106383        .319149       ‾.2978724
‾.2978723      .106383        .2340425
```

(b)   Restructuring functions

These act solely on the structure and not on the content; the result is formed from all or part of the elements of the operand. The effects of these functions can be either to modify completely the initial structure of the right operand, to add to or remove elements, or finally to change completely the arrangement of the constituent elements.

(b.1)   Structure modification

As we saw when we learnt how to construct arrays, the relevant function here is the dyadic ρ. One of the most frequent operations is the transformation of an array into a vector. This is possible with the above function. However, there is a special function of linearisation, the ravel function (moving from n dimensions to 1), symbolised by a comma, which allows the operation to be written more simply.

```
      M←5 4ρ'INCONSEQUENTIAL'
      M
INCO
NSEQ
UENT
IALI
NCON

      M←5 3ρ

      M←5 3ρ'INCONSEQUENTIAL
      M
INC
ONS
EQU
ENT
IAL

      (×/ρM)ρM
INCONSEQUENTIAL
      ,M
INCONSEQUENTIAL
```

(b.2)   Addition or deletion of elements

   Catenation. This is the operation that joins two structures together.
Thus, if V1 and V2 designate two vectors of the same type, linking them
together gives a vector composed of the elements of V1, followed by those of
V2. The corresponding function in APL is the dyadic comma.

   For example:

```
        V1←'DEAR LADY '
        V2←'YOUR SOFT EYES '
        V3←'MAKE ME '
        V4←'SWOON '
        V5←'WITH LOVE '
        V1,V2,V3,V4,V5
DEAR LADY YOUR SOFT EYES MAKE ME SWOON WITH LOVE
        V5,V4,V1,V2,V3
WITH LOVE SWOON DEAR LADY YOUR SOFT EYES MAKE ME
        V2,V5,V3,V1,V4
YOUR SOFT EYES WITH LOVE MAKE ME DEAR LADY SWOON
```

If we want to link together structures of higher rank, then we must specify the
dimension along which the catenation should operate. If M1 and M2 represent
two matrices, the expression M1,[1]M2 means that catenation takes place along
their first dimension, that is to say along the rows (providing the dimensions are
compatible).

```
        M1←2 4ρ1
        M2←3 4ρ2
        M3←2 3ρ3
        M1,[1]M2
1   1   1   1
1   1   1   1
2   2   2   2
2   2   2   2
2   2   2   2

        M1,[2]M3
1   1   1   1   3   3   3
1   1   1   1   3   3   3
```

If the dimension is not specified, the catenation takes place along the last one
(or the columns in the case of a matrix).

   Compression. This enables the elements in a structure to be deleted. The
corresponding function (/) is dyadic. Its left operand is a logic vector which
specifies what is to be retained (1) and what is to be deleted (0).

```
        1 1 1 0 0 1 1 1/'PANORAMA'
PANAMA
```

The following problems can be solved simply by compression.

Select the positive elements in a vector:

```
      V
34  ‾33  32   8  ‾29   1  ‾18  37  33   2
      (V≥0)/V
34   32   8   1   37  33   2
```

Delete the spaces in a piece of text:

```
      (V≠' ')/V←' I T I S  F I N E'
ITISFINE
```

Equally, it is used to carry out branching operations in functions. The expression:

```
      →V/E1,E2,E3,E4,E5
```

causes a branching at the first label of the compressed vector. If V is only composed of 0s, the compression results in an empty vector, and we continue in sequence. To compress a matrix, the dimension to be reduced must be indicated.

```
      M
12   5    4    14
10   13   10   17
20   13   11   12
          1  0  1  1/[2]M
12   4    14
10   10   17
20   11   12
          1  0  1/[1]M
12   5    4    14
20   13   11   12
```

Expansion. This is the opposite operation to compression: it inserts new elements in the structure. If the latter is numerical, the elements inserted are 0s. If it is of the character type, then the elements are spaces.

```
      1  1  1  0  1\[2]M
12   5    4    0    14
10   13   10   0    17
20   13   11   0    12


      1  1  0  1  1  0  1  1  1  1\'ITISFINE'
IT IS FINE
```

For all these functions, the same convention is adopted, and, if the dimension is not explicitly specified, the function acts on the last dimension. Finally, there are special symbols equivalent to /[1] and \[1]: these are $\neq$ and $\curlywedge$ derived by overstriking / and — or \ and —.

Take and drop. These dyadic functions are symbolised by ↑ and ↓ respectively.

If V is a vector the expression N↑V (N takes V) takes the first N elements of V if N is positive, and the last —N elements if N is negative.

The opposite operation is 'drop'; N↓V gives a vector formed from the elements of V dropping the first N elements (or dropping the last —N elements if N is negative).

```
      4↑V←'OVERRATED'
OVER
      ‾5↑V
RATED
```

```
      4↓7↑V
RAT
```

When N is greater than ρV, N↑V gives a vector supplemented with 0s or spaces depending on what type of vector V is. This is its subtle difference from the dyadic function ρ.

```
      10↑ι4
1   2   3   4   0   0   0   0   0   0
      10ρι4
1   2   3   4   1   2   3   4   1   2
```

These functions apply equally to arrays. The left operand indicates what should be taken or left in each dimension.

	M			
1	2	3	4	5
6	7	8	9	10
11	0	0	12	13
14	0	0	15	16
17	18	19	20	21

Extracting the null submatrix is carried out very easily:

```
      2 1↓4 3↑M
```

```
0   0
0   0
```

(b.3)   Rearrangement

There are three operations in APL that bring about changes in the elemental arrangement within a structure. These are reversal, rotation, and transposition.

Reversal. This consists of reversing the arrangement of the elements of the dimension specified or of the last one if the dimension is not specified. The function is a monadic one. It is symbolised by φ (derived from o and |).

```
        φι4
4    3    2    1
        φ'STAR'
RATS
        M
7    3    8    10
2    11   9    12
1    4    5    6
        φ[1]M
1    4    5    6
2    11   9    12
7    3    8    10

     φM
10   8    3    7
12   9    11   2
6    5    4    1
```

The symbol ⊖ (derived from o and -) is equivalent to φ[1].

Rotation. This is the dyadic form of the above function. The left operand specifies the order of the rotation. When it is positive, the elements are displaced in descending order of indexes, and in ascending order when negative.

```
        1φ'NEAR'
EARN
        2φ'MITRE'
TREMI
```

```
        2φ[1]M
1    4    5    6
7    3    8    10
2    11   9    12
          2 0 ¯1 5φ[1]M
1    3    5    6
7    11   8    10
2    4    9    12
```

Transposition. An array is transposed by the function ⍉. If the array is a matrix, the rows and columns are transposed.

```
        M
7    3    8    10
2    11   9    12
1    4    5    6

        ⍉M
7    2    1
3    11   4
8    9    5
10   12   6
```

(c)   *Mixed functions*

The structure of the resulting array is in general different from that of the operands. Its content is the result of a calculation.

Reduction, inner product and outer product enable some problems to be solved very easily; for example, finding the smallest element of an array, or the product of two matrices, etc.

Reduction. We saw earlier how this can be applied to vectors. It can also be extended to arrays of any rank, but the dimension along which it operates must be specified. This dimension disappears in the result.

```
        M
7    3    8    10
2    11   9    12
1    4    5    6
```

To sum the elements of each row:

```
        +/M
28   34   16
```

To sum the elements of each column:

```
        +⌿M
10   18   22   28
```

To sum all the elements of the matrix:

```
        +/+/M
78
```

Inner product. This enables two dyadic scalar functions to be applied between two operands. If V and W are two vectors and f and g two dyadic functions, the inner product is written:

$$R \leftarrow Vf.gW$$

and its result is given by:

$$R = (V_1 g W_1)f \dots f(V_n g W_n)$$

Figure 3 gives a schematic representation of the operation in process.

If M and N are matrices or arrays of rank greater than 2, the last coordinate of M should have the same number of elements as the first coordinate of N; in the case:

$$Mf . gN$$

the dimension of the result is the catenation of the other coordinates of M and N.

Figure 4 represents schematically the algorithm of the inner product of two matrices:

$$R_{ij} = (M_{i1}gN_{1j})f(M_{i2}gN_{2j})f \ldots f(M_{in}gN_{nj})$$

Thus we take the inner product of each possible combination of pairs of vectors corresponding to a row of M with a column of N. We are reminded of the earlier example of vectors.

If the dimensions of M and N are (a, b) and (b, c) respectively the dimensions of the result are (a,c).

$$R \leftarrow M + . \times N$$

gives a result:

$$R_{ij} = \sum_{k} M_{ik} \times N_{kj}$$

The result, in this case, corresponds to the familiar matrix product (Figure 5).

Figure 3

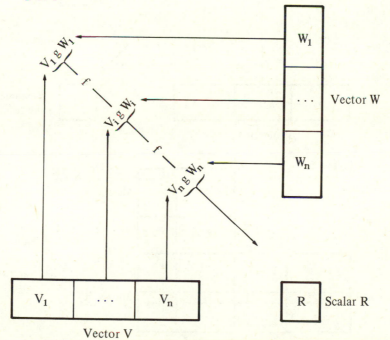

Vector V

Example

```
M+.×⊞M←2 2ρι4
1          0
0           .9999998
```

Thus, the product of a matrix with its inverse gives, contrary to appearances, the identity matrix.

The precision of the representation of the numbers in the memory, and the precision of the calculations involved in inversion are limited. This is why there

Figure 4

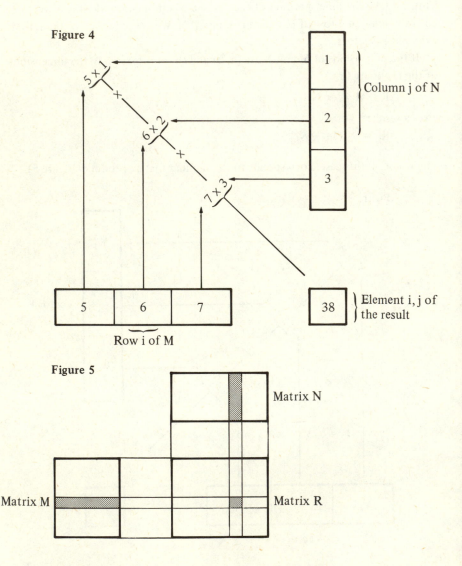

Column j of N

Row i of M

Element i, j of the result

Figure 5

Matrix N

Matrix M

Matrix R

were not just 0s and 1s given in the solution. Other dyadic functions can be called into play in the inner product. For example, to find out if a string of characters is identical to one of the rows of an array NAMES we simply write:

```
      NAMES
TABLE
SABLE
MABLE
MAPLE
APPLE
      NAMES∧.='SABLE'
0  1  0  0  0
      NAMES∧.='CABLE'
0  0  0  0  0
```

If we want to know if a certain string of characters exists in a matrix it is sufficient to reduce by union the resultant vector obtained:

```
      ∨/NAMES∧.='SABLE'
1

      ∨/NAMES∧.='CABLE'
0
```

Outer product. This allows a dyadic scalar function to be applied between arrays. The operation is carried out between each element of one operand and each element of the other. If V and W are vectors and f is a dyadic scalar function, the outer product is denoted:

$$R \leftarrow V \circ . f W$$

and its result is a matrix of dimensions (ρV), (ρW) with a general term of the form:

$$R_{ij} = V_i f W_j$$

For example a multiplication table is written:

```
      (ι5)∘.×ι6
1     2     3     4     5     6
2     4     6     8     10    12
3     6     9     12    15    18
4     8     12    16    20    24
5     10    15    20    25    30
```

Figure 6 is a schematic representation of this calculation. Without exception, the dimension of the result is the catenation of the dimensions of the two operands. Thus the outer product extends to any operand, whatever its rank and dimension. Generally, then, if V1 and V2 are the dimensions of M1 and M2 in:

$$R \leftarrow M1 \circ . f M2$$

the dimensions of R are (V1,V2) and each element of R is given by:

$$R_{i_1 i_2 \ldots i_m i_{m+1} \ldots i_{m+n}} = M1_{i_1 i_2 \ldots i_m} \, f \, M2_{i_1 \ldots i_n}$$

with:

$$m = \rho V1$$

$$n = \rho V2$$

Suppose we want to find out how many times the different vowels appear in a piece of text.

```
VOWELS←'AEIOU'
TEXT←'AN EXAMPLE OF OUTER PRODUCT'
```

We simply write the outer product:

```
VOWELS∘.=TEXT
```

The result is a matrix in which the first row indicates the positions of the first vowel in TEXT:

```
1 0 0 0 0 1 0 0 0 0 0 0 0 0 0 0 0 0 0 0 0 0 0 0 0 0 0
0 0 0 1 0 0 0 0 0 0 1 0 0 0 0 0 0 0 1 0 0 0 0 0 0 0 0
0 0 0 0 0 0 0 0 0 0 0 0 0 0 0 0 0 0 0 0 0 0 0 0 0 0 0
0 0 0 0 0 0 0 0 0 0 0 1 0 0 1 0 0 0 0 0 0 0 1 0 0 0 0
0 0 0 0 0 0 0 0 0 0 0 0 0 0 0 1 0 0 0 0 0 0 0 0 1 0 0
```

Figure 6

X	1 2	3	4 5	6
1				
2				
3		9		18
4				
5				

Now all that remains to be done is to reduce this matrix by summation of the rows to obtain the desired result:

```
      +/VOWELS∘.=TEXT
2   3   0   3   2
```

It is possible to write very concise expressions using the inner and outer products, as the following two functions illustrate:

```
     ∇ HISTO V
[1]    (⌽ι⌈/V)∘.≤V
     ∇

     ∇ X CRV Y
[1]    ((⌽ι⌈/Y)∘.=Y)∨.∧X∘.=ι⌈/X
     ∇
```

HISTO calculates a histogram given in vector form by V. CRV computes a curve defined point by point: the first value of Y is linked to the first value of X. The operands of these two functions are vectors of the integer type. The result is given in the form of a matrix: each element is equal to 1 if it forms part of the histogram (or curve), otherwise it is equal to 0.

```
        HISTO 3 4 5 7 5 0 3 5 1
0 0 0 1 0 0 0 0 0
0 0 0 1 0 0 0 0 0
0 0 1 1 1 0 0 1 0
0 1 1 1 1 0 0 1 0
1 1 1 1 1 0 1 1 0
1 1 1 1 1 0 1 1 0
1 1 1 1 1 0 1 1 1

        5 3 1 2 6 4 CRV 5 2 4 3 2 4
0 0 0 0 1 0
1 0 0 1 0 0
0 1 0 0 0 0
0 0 1 0 0 1
0 0 0 0 0 0
```

The interpretation of these computations is left to the insight of the reader!

4.4   Indices

So far we have only handled objects as a whole (constant, vector, matrix, ...), without worrying about the individual components. In certain cases it might be necessary to access the elements of an array. This is achieved by using *indices* – positive integers that indicate the *position* of the element (or elements) relative to the first element of the array. The index can be of any structure (scalar, vector, matrix ...) and gives its structure to the result. These indices are placed inside square brackets behind the array to be indexed. Let us look at some examples to see how to carry out the indexing.

```
      V←2  5  9  14  25
      V[2]
5
      VL5  1  2]
25    2    5
      V[ι3] ◄─────────────────────── (Equivalent here to 3↑V)
2     5    9
      V[1.4]
DOMAIN ERROR ◄───────────────────── Non-integer index
      V[1.4]
        ∧
      V[6]
INDEX ERROR ◄─────────────────── Index greater than the dimension
      V[6]
        ∧
```

```
      'ARST'[4  4ρ2  1  4  3  4  3  1  2  3  4  1  2  1  2  4  3]
RATS
TSAR
STAR
ARTS
```

If we consider the example of the histogram cited in the previous section we notice that we would obtain a matrix composed of 0s and 1s. Such a matrix can in fact be used as an index to trace a histogram:

```
      ∇ HISTO V
[1]     ' □'[1+(φι⌈/V)∘.≤V]
      ∇
      HISTO  3  5  4  7  5  0  3  5  1
```

```
      □
      □
  □ □□   □
  □□□□   □
□□□□□ □□
□□□□□ □□
□□□□□ □□□
```

Notice that 1 had to be added to the index matrix since the space is the element of index 1 (and not 0) of the vector to be indexed.

In the same way we can trace a curve using a function based on CRV cited in 4.3:

```
     ∇  X  CRV  Y
[1]     '  *'[1+((ϕι⌈/Y)∘.=Y)∨.∧X∘.=ι⌈/X]
     ∇

         16  12  4  8  2  6  10  14  CRV  3  5  4  7  2  6  6  4
              *
          *      *
          -
                    *
     *            *
                      *

 *
```

In arrays of rank greater than or equal to 2, an element is referenced by as many indices as there are dimensions. These indices are separated by a semi-colon:

```
     M←4  3ρι12
     M
1    2    3
4    5    6
7    8    9
10   11   12
     M[2;3]
6
     M[2;ι3]
4    5    6
     M[1 3;2 3]
2    3
8    9
```

Suppose we want to obtain the second row of the matrix M. We can write:

```
     M[2;ι3]
4    5    6
```

and more generally:

```
     M[2;ι(ρM)[2]]
4    5    6

     M[2;ι1↓ρM]
4    5    6
```

which is, all the same, rather cumbersome!

There is a simpler expression that will give the same result; it is assumed that when no index is specified for a particular dimension, then *all* the indices relating to that dimension are required:

```
     M[2;]
4    5    6  ◄─────────────────────────
```
Elements of the second row and of all the columns

```
     M[;3]
3    6    9    12 ◄─────────────────────
```
Elements of the third column and all the rows

4.5 Modification of the elements of an array

Obviously any element can be changed once it can be identified within an array.

```
V←ι10
V[3 5 9]←57
V
1   2   57   4   57   6   7   8   57   10


M←?3 10ρ100
M
84   17   82   58   21   51   32   87   83
50   6    93   55   32   26   22   43   26
93   52   29   51   76   65   87   26   95


M[2;]←V
M
84   17   82   58   21   51   32   87   83
1    2    57   4    57   6    7    8    57
93   52   29   51   76   65   87   26   95
```

4.6 Index search in a vector

So far we have learnt how to access the elements of an array. Now we are concerned with the examination by 'context' of certain elements. Consider the following:

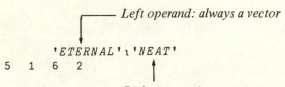

Left operand: always a vector

```
'ETERNAL'ι'NEAT'
5   1   6   2
```

Right operand: any structure

The series of values obtained corresponds to the index of the letters of ETERNAL from which the word NEAT can be constructed. Thus the first element of NEAT is the fifth element of ETERNAL and so on. Thus:

```
'ETERNAL'['ETERNAL'ι'NEAT']
NEAT
```

The function used to perform this index search is the dyadic 'iota'. It can be applied equally well to numbers and characters.

```
13 22 1ι4 2ρ13 1 22 1 1 13 1 2
1   3
2   3
3   1
3   2
```

If an element of the right operand does not exist in the left operand, the result is an index greater by 1 than the number of elements of the left operand. Thus:

```
      'INTERN' ι 'NEAT'
2   4   7   3
```
————————————————— *This element does not*
————————————————————————————————— *exist*

4.7   Index origin

We have remarked that the smallest index used has the value 1. This is a convention that can be changed explicitly by modifying the system variable □IO:

$$\Box IO \leftarrow \langle N \rangle$$

with $\langle N \rangle = 0$ or 1, 1 being the implicit origin.

It is important to notice that index origin relates not only to indexing but also to certain functions such as ? or ι. For example:

```
      □IO
1
      □IO←0
      ι5
0   1   2   3   4

      □IO←1
      ι5
1   2   3   4   5
```

In particular the expression:

$$\rightarrow \langle label \rangle \times \iota \langle condition \rangle$$

takes, with 0 as the origin, the meaning:

If the condition is true, then leave the function, if not continue in sequence

In other words, the label is no longer of any use!

4.8   Important points

Rank:	*number of dimensions*;
Monadic functions:	ρ ⊟, ϕ ⊖;
Dyadic functions:	ρ , ι / \ ϕ ⊖ ↑ ↓;
Generalised products:	{ inner: g . g; outer: ° . g;
Indexing:	[i; j; ...];
Index origin:	□IO.

5   FURTHER FUNCTIONS

5.1   Communicating with the outside world – input/output

We have already seen the different ways in which the user communicates via the terminal with the APL system. In particular we have seen that the result of a calculation will not be displayed at the terminal if it is assigned to a variable. Thus with:

```
    ι10
1   2   3   4   5   6   7   8   9   10
```

a result is displayed, but with:

```
    A←ι10
```

no result is displayed.

A special variable, □ (called quad), represents the terminal in use. This variable is used in the same way as an ordinary variable; it can in particular be read or specified. Thus:

```
    □←A←ι10
1   2   3   4   5   6   7   8   9   10
```

displays a specified result, while:

```
    A←ι□
□:
    7
```

asks for a value to be read from the terminal. Once this value has been entered:

```
    A
1   2   3   4   5   6   7
```

a result is supplied.

Every time the APL interpreter meets the character □ in an input statement, it prints □:, goes to the beginning of a new line and moves the carriage forward six spaces.

We can construct more complicated expressions:

```
      M←(□,2)ρ□
□:
      ι10
□:
      3
      M
1   2
3   4
5   6
```

We can see how, by using □, we can enter any expression which is then calculated immediately.

```
      A←□+3
□:
      2×4
      A
11
```

In the same way

```
      □←A←'ABCD'
ABCD
      A←□
□:
      'XYZ'
      A
XYZ
```

Another special variable, ⍞ called quote-quad (derived from the characters ⍞ and) can also be used. In this case the lines entered are treated as strings of characters and are not evaluated. In output, the carriage remains positioned behind the last printed character.

```
      ⍞←'1+2'
1+2
```

is identical to

```
      □←'1+2'
1+2
```

except that the carriage remains positioned behind the 2 in the case of ⍞; this means that several data items can be printed on the same line.

The differences between □ and ⍞ are as follows depending on whether they are in input (with the variable on the right hand side of an expression) or in output (specifying this variable):

In input (to the right of the specification arrow)

⍞: does not print any prompt and takes the input line as a string of characters.

□: prints the prompt '□:' and evaluates the line entered.

The function of ⊡ in input can be more complex in certain APL systems.

In output (to the left of the specification arrow)

□ moves to the next line after every specification, which is not the case
with ⊡. However the two variables can take values of any type.

We can therefore write functions that permit interaction with the user the moment they are activated.

Consider a bank that offers accounts to its clients at different interest rates and suppose we wanted to write a function that calculates the final capital, given the initial capital, an interest rate and the number of years. This function can be written:

```
    ∇ RES←INTEREST1 A
[1]    ⋒A = CAPITAL RATE YEAR
[2]    RES←A[1]×(A[2]+1)*A[3]
    ∇
```

The character ⋒ (∩ and °), called comment, indicates that the text situated to the right is a comment which will help clarify an obscure expression.

```
    INTEREST1 1000 .05 1
1050
    INTEREST1 1000 .1 3
1331
```

In this case it is difficult to use this function 'conversationally', especially for users not familiar with it. We suggest defining a function that will guide the user:

```
    ∇ INTEREST
[1]    'PROGRAM FOR CAPITAL CALCULATION'
[2]    ⎕←'  INITIAL CAPITAL ?'
[3]    CAP←⎕
[4]    ⎕←'  ANNUAL RATE OF INTEREST ?'
[5]    RATE←⎕
[6]    ⎕←'  DURATION OF CAPITALIZATION ?'
[7]    YEAR←⎕
[8]    'FINAL CAPITAL = ';CAP×(RATE+1)*YEAR
    ∇

    INTEREST
PROGRAM FOR CAPITAL CALCULATION
□:INITIAL CAPITAL ?
    1000
□:ANNUAL RATE OF INTEREST ?
    .1
□:DURATION OF CAPITALIZATION ?
    3
FINAL CAPITAL = 1331
```

The symbol ; (on line 8) enables mixed output (that is to say results of any type) to be printed on the same line.

Suppose we wanted to test the validity of the values entered by the user for the function INTEREST. The range of these values should be:

(a)   for the capital, a positive number;

(b)   for the rate, a positive number between 0 and 1;

(c)   for the number of years, strictly a positive integer.

Consider the case of the capital: after **CAP** has been specified, its value must be tested, and if it is found to be negative, then another value is requested. The branching function → is used for this. Remember that this function applies to a value that can be the result of any expression. In this case line 2 of the function must be re-executed if the data typed in is incorrect, otherwise execution proceeds to line 4. Thus,

```
      ∇INTEREST[3.5]
[3.5] →(CAP≤0)/2
[3.6] ∇
```

Let us demonstrate:

```
      INTEREST
PROGRAM FOR CAPITAL CALCULATION
□:INITIAL CAPITAL ?
      ¯3
□:INITIAL CAPITAL ?
   10000
□:ANNUAL RATE OF INTEREST ?
   .1
□:DURATION OF CAPITALIZATION ?
   1
FINAL CAPITAL = 11000
```

The branching test on line 2 depends on the result of the operation $(CAP \leq 0)$. In fact, recalling the compression function, we have

```
      (¯2≤0)/2
2
```

and

```
      (3≤0)/2
```

In the one case there is a branching to line 2, and in the other case, since the result is an empty vector, by convention the operator → is not effective and execution continues in sequence.

Let us now modify the function, in order to carry out other tests:

```
     ∇ INTEREST
[1]    'PROGRAM FOR CAPITAL CALCULATION'
[2]    ▯←' INITIAL CAPITAL ?'
[3]    CAP←▯
[4]    →(CAP≤0)/2
[5]    ▯←' ANNUAL RATE OF INTEREST ?'
[6]    RATE←▯
[7]    →((RATE≤0)∨RATE≥1)/5
[8]    ▯←' DURATION OF CAPITALIZATION ?'
[9]    YEAR←▯
[10]   →((YEAR≤0)∨YEAR≠⌊YEAR)/8
[11]   'FINAL CAPITAL = ';CAP×(RATE+1)*YEAR
     ∇
```

Note that the lines have been renumbered. We can see from this the advantage in using labels. Let us carry out the tests on the function:

```
     INTEREST
PROGRAM FOR CAPITAL CALCULATION
▯:INITIAL CAPITAL ?
      ‾10
▯:INITIAL CAPITAL ?
      1000
▯:ANNUAL RATE OF INTEREST ?
      1.2
▯:ANNUAL RATE OF INTEREST ?
      .1
▯:DURATION OF CAPITALIZATION ?
      2.8
▯:DURATION OF CAPITALIZATION ?
      ‾20
▯:DURATION OF CAPITALIZATION ?
      3
FINAL CAPITAL = 1331
```

5.2 Transformation of type

Now consider:

```
     X←5
     'X EQUALS ',X
DOMAIN ERROR
     'X EQUALS ',X
              ∧
```

In fact, it is impossible to catenate a variable of the 'numerical' type to a variable of the 'character' type. There are however functions which can transform a variable of one type to that of another. We shall only consider here the function that transforms numerical vectors to character vectors. This is the function ▼

(called enquote derived from ○ (upper shift J) and T). The function which carries out the opposite operation is the 'dequote' (⍕) or 'execute' function which we shall study later, since it possesses properties supplementary to those of a simple transformation of type. Thus:

```
      □←'X EQUALS ',▼X
X EQUALS 5
```

Let us verify it:

```
      ρX
      ←─────────────── Empty vector
      ρ▼X
3
```

In fact, the expression ⊤X adds two spaces after the character 5.

5.3   Iteration

We are now going to write a function that can define words and arrange them in a matrix. It is important to notice that every word in the matrix must be of the same length, for example 8. Let WORDS be such a function, and N the number of words.

```
      ∇ RES←WORDS N
[1]     X←'' ⍝ IX IS AN EMPTY VECTOR
[2]     I←N ⍝ MAXIMUM NUMBER OF WORDS
[3]     X←X,8↑□ ⍝ APPEND OF A NEW WORD
[4]     I←I-1 ⍝UPDATE NUMBER OF WORDS
[5]     →(I>0)/3 ⍝ CONTINUES
[6]     RES←(N,8)ρX ⍝ REDIMENSIONS X TO A MARIX N×8
      ∇
```

Let us call such a function:

```
      ENGLISH←WORDS 5
CAT
DOG
MOUSE
RHINOCEROS
DUCK

      ENGLISH
CAT
DOG
MOUSE
RHINOCER
DUCK
```

Suppose we made a mistake with the number of words to be entered (too many for example) and we wanted to exit from the loop without having to type

in the whole set of words demanded. We could interrupt an input by superimposing the characters O U T. Thus:

```
        WORDS 5200
TOTO
TUTU
OUT
▨
WORDS[3] *
        →
```

However we could have created a function that terminates when an empty
line is typed in (using the carriage return key). Let WORDS1 be such a function:

```
      ∇ RES←WORDS1
[1]    X←'' ⍝ X IS AN EMPTY VECTOR
[2]    N←0 ⍝ NUMBER OF WORDS ENTERED
[3]    SEQUENCE:→(0=ρY←▯)/END ⍝ READS A WORD, STOP IF EMPT
[4]    X←X,8↑Y
[5]    N←N+1
[6]    →SEQUENCE
[7]    END:RES←(N,8)ρX ⍝ RESTRUCTRUES THE WORDS VECTOR
      ∇
        WORDS1
GOOD DAY
HELLO
GOOD BYE

GOOD DAY
HELLO
GOOD BYE
```

5.4   Decoding and encoding

How many seconds are there in a day? This is an extremely simple
problem to resolve. All that we need do is type in at the terminal
24 60 60 ⊥ 24 0 0.

```
      24 60 60 ⊥ 24 0 0
86400
```

The base of the numerical vector to be decoded is expressed to the left of ⊥
and the vector to be decoded is expressed to the right. The result is the value to
base 10 of the vector to be decoded. If B is the vector to be decoded ($\rho B = 3$),
and if A is the base ($\rho A = 3$), then the result of $A \perp B$ is:

$$B(3)$$
$$+ B(2) \times A(3)$$
$$+ B(1) \times A(3) \times A(2)$$

Notice that A(1) is not involved in any of the calculations and is only there so that the dimensions are respected.

```
      1  60  60  ⊥  24  0  0
86400
```

This example is trivial since we only needed to write 3600 × 24, but we could also write:

```
      24  60  60  ⊥  12  34  56  ←──────────── Number of seconds in
45296                                          12 hr 34 min 56 s
         10  ⊥  1  9  7  5
1975
```

Notice that in this last example 10 has been extended to the dimension of the vector 1,9,7,5.

Let us make the problem slightly more complex by introducing a matrix on the right.

```
      A←3  4ρ1  9  7  5  19

      A←3  4ρ1  9  7  5  1  9  7  6  1  9  7  7
      A
1    9    7    5
1    9    7    6
1    9    7    7
         10  ⊥  A
111    999    777    567
```

We do not obtain exactly the result anticipated. However, all we need do is transpose the matrix.

```
      10  ⊥  ⍉A
1975    1976    1977
```

The function 'encode' (T) executes the inverse function; if we want to know what 1234 seconds is in hours, minutes and seconds, we can type in at the terminal:

```
      24  60  60  ⊤  1234
0    20    34
```

The result of A T B is the number B in base A, A and B being numerical. More generally, B can be a vector or a matrix. The result of A T B has the dimensions $(\rho A), \rho B$ with $(\rho A) \leqslant 1$ (vector or scalar).

The following example gives the binary representation of the integers between 0 and 15.

```
    (0,ι15),⍴2 2 2 2⊤0,ι15
0    0    0    0    0
1    0    0    0    1
2    0    0    1    0
3    0    0    1    1
4    0    1    0    0
5    0    1    0    1
6    0    1    1    0
7    0    1    1    1
8    1    0    0    0
9    1    0    0    1
10   1    0    1    0
11   1    0    1    1
12   1    1    0    0
13   1    1    0    1
14   1    1    1    0
15   1    1    1    1
```

5.5   Sorting

Let NAME be an array containing 10 names of workers in a company. Let NAS be an array of 10 rows corresponding to the 10 workers and 3 columns corresponding to:

> the number of children;
>
> the age;
>
> the monthly salary of each worker.

The problem consists of editing these two arrays relative to each other, the rows being sorted in ascending order of the combination of these three criteria:

> N for the number of children;
>
> A for age;
>
> S for salary.

Thus, if the key to the sorting, AS, is supplied, this means that the array should be edited in order of age, and, age being equal, in order of salary.

```
      NAME
 ARTHUR
 HECTOR
 JULIAN
 PAUL
 SIMON
 JOHN
 ROBERT
 HENRY
 CHARLES
 HUGH
```

	NAS	
0	2 3	1200
1	2 5	1300
3	2 4	1200
0	2 4	1400
5	2 6	1200
0	2 9	1400
1	2 4	1200
4	2 5	1400
2	2 3	1500
3	2 9	1400

The idea is to obtain one column of numbers from the three columns (number
of children, age and salary, catenated in a certain order) and to sort this column
in ascending order printing the arrays NAME and NAS indexed by the result of
the sort.

The column of numbers is obtained by saying that the three columns of NAS
correspond to values in a certain base. This base should be greater than all the
NAS numbers to remove any possibility of problems. Take for example 2000.
Then NAS is decoded whilst ensuring that the three NAS columns are permu-
tated according to the sort key supplied by the user, in such a way that the first
criterion (the major criterion) appears on the left, the second in the middle, and
the third on the right.

To carry out this sort, we use the function $\spadesuit$ (derived from the characters
$\triangle$ and |). This function applied to a vector V provides the vector of indices
which allows V to be classed in ascending order:

```
      ▲ V←3  2  5  1851  14
2   1   3   5   4
```

```
      V[▲V]
2   3   5   14   1851
```

The descending sort is made by the operator ψ.

```
      ∇ MULTSORT
[1]      ⍝ SAMPLE OF MULTIPLE SORT
[2]      'SORT KEY PLEASE ( COMBINATION OF LETTERS N A S) ?'
[3]      (NAME,▼NAS)[▲2000⊥⍉NAS[;,3↑('NAS'⍳⍞),1 2 3];]
      ∇
```

```
      MULTSORT
SORT KEY PLEASE ( COMBINATION OF LETTERS N A S) ?
NAS
ARTHUR   0      23      1200
PAUL     0      24      1400
JOHN     0      29      1400
```

```
ROBERT    1      24      1200
HECTOR    1      25      1300
CHARLES   2      23      1500
JULIAN    3      24      1200
HUGH      3      29      1400
HENRY     4      25      1400
SIMON     5      26      1200

        MULTSORT
SORT KEY PLEASE ( COMBINATION OF LETTERS N A S) ?
SA
ARTHUR    0      23      1200
JULIAN    3      24      1200
SIMON     5      26      1200
ROBERT    1      24      1200
HECTOR    1      25      1300
PAUL      0      24      1400
JOHN      0      29      1400
HENRY     4      25      1400
HUGH      3      29      1400
CHARLES   2      23      1500
```

5.6   Membership

In APL we can test if the elements of an object (numerical or alphabetical) belong to a set of other elements of the same type; the right and left operands can be of any structure. If we want to know the set of characters in the word 'CHAT' contained in the word 'CAT' we can write:

```
      'CHAT' ε 'CAT'
1 0 1 1
```

which signifies that the first, third and fourth characters of the left operand exist in the right operand.

The result of the membership function is of the logic type, its structure being that of the left operand.

```
      'CHAT' ε3 5
DOMAIN ERROR
      'CHAT'ε3 5
           ∧
      3 2 4 5 ε 3 2ρ4
0 0 1 0
      (2 3ρ4 3 2 1 10 18) ε 5 10ρ18
1 1 1
1 0 0
```

Operands of the same type but of any structure

5.7   Execute function

Let us write a program to assist in teaching APL. For example, if we take the function:

```
      ∇ EVAL
[1]     'IN APL EXPRESSIONS ARE EVALUATED FROM RIGHT'
[2]     'TO LEFT WITH NO PRIORITY BETWEEN FUNCTIONS'
[3]     'FOR EXAMPLE 3×2+1 GIVES : ';3×2+1
[4]     'TRY IT. TYPE IN AN APL EXPRESSION :'
[5]     A←□
[6]     'GIVE THE RESULT OF YOUR EXPRESSION :'
[7]     B←□
[8]     □←(2 5ρ'RIGHTWRONG')[1+A≠B;]
      ∇
```

Let us try:

```
      EVAL
IN APL EXPRESSIONS ARE EVALUATED FROM RIGHT
TO LEFT WITH NO PRIORITY BETWEEN FUNCTIONS
FOR EXAMPLE 3×2+1 GIVES : 9
TRY IT. TYPE IN AN APL EXPRESSION :
□:
      1+2÷3-4
GIVE THE RESULT OF YOUR EXPRESSION :
□:
      21
WRONG
```

The function works. However, we can soon see that it is easy to cheat, for example by typing the same expression twice.

```
      EVAL
IN APL EXPRESSIONS ARE EVALUATED FROM RIGHT
TO LEFT WITH NO PRIORITY BETWEEN FUNCTIONS
FOR EXAMPLE 3×2+1 GIVES : 9
TRY IT. TYPE IN AN APL EXPRESSION :
□:
      1+2÷3-4
GIVE THE RESULT OF YOUR EXPRESSION :
□:
      1+2÷3-4
RIGHT
```

Notice that in learning how to cheat one also learns how quad operates. Suppose that we wanted to train ourselves in mental arithmetic, restricting ourselves to expressions that contain only the following operators: $+ - × ÷$. Furthermore, we want the reply to be solely numerical. For this we need to use a new function (called 'dequote' or 'execute') derived from the characters ∘ (upper shift J) and ⊥.

A string of characters can be evaluated using this function. For example:

```
      ⍎'1+2'
3
      A←'1+1'
      ⍎A
2
```

The sequence ⍕ ⎕ is the same as ⎕, except for the printing of the prompt.

The teaching program can now be written:

```
      ∇ EVAL
[1]    'IN APL EXPRESSIONS ARE EVALUATED FROM RIGHT'
[2]    'TO LEFT WITH NO PRIORITY BETWEEN FUNCTIONS'
[3]    'FOR EXAMPLE 3×2+1 GIVES : ';3×2+1
[4]    'TRY IT. TYPE IN AN ARITHMETIC EXPRESSION'
[5]    'JUST USING THE FUNCTIONS +,-,×,÷'
[6]    TEST1:→((⌈/(ALPHA←'¯0123456789.+-×÷')
         ⍳A←⎕)∈13 14 15 16)/GOON
[7]    'INCORRECT EXPRESSION'
[8]    →TEST1
[9]    GOON:'GIVE THE RESULT OF YOUR EXPRESSION :'
[10]   →END×13>⌈/ALPHA⍳B←⎕
[11]   'INCORRECT REPLY '
[12]   →GOON
[13]   END:(2 5ρ'RIGHTWRONG')[1+(⍎A)≠⍎B;]
[14]   'TRY AGAIN'
[15]   →TEST1
      ∇
```

Line 6 defines the alphabet ALPHA and verifies that A only contains characters of ALPHA, of which at least one is one of the four functions.

Line 10 checks that B is a numerical constant.

Line 13 verifies that A and B give the same result.

```
      EVAL
IN APL EXPRESSIONS ARE EVALUATED FROM RIGHT
TO LEFT WITH NO PRIORITY BETWEEN FUNCTIONS
FOR EXAMPLE 3×2+1 GIVES : 9
TRY IT. TYPE IN AN ARITHMETIC EXPRESSION
JUST USING THE FUNCTIONS +,-,×,÷
1-2-3-4
GIVE THE RESULT OF YOUR EXPRESSION :
¯2
RIGHT
TRY AGAIN
1÷2+3
GIVE THE RESULT OF YOUR EXPRESSION :
0,2
INCORRECT REPLY
GIVE THE RESULT OF YOUR EXPRESSION :
0000.20
RIGHT
TRY AGAIN
1/2 8,9
INCORRECT EXPRESSION
1+2+3+4
GIVE THE RESULT OF YOUR EXPRESSION :
1+2+3+4
INCORRECT REPLY
GIVE THE RESULT OF YOUR EXPRESSION :
▨
EVAL[10] ★
      →
```

The following final example illustrates another use of the function execute.

Suppose that within the function F we wanted, depending on the result of the calculation of I, to call one of the following four functions: F1, F2, F3, or F4. A possible solution is:

```
     ∇ F I
[1]     →(E1,E2,E3,E4)[I]
[2]    E1:F1
[3]     →0
[4]    E2:F2
[5]     →0
[6]    E3:F3
[7]     →0
[8]    E4:F4
[9]     →0
     ∇
```

With the function execute, these call instructions can be resolved quite easily:

```
     ∇ F I
[1]    ⍕'F','1234'[I]
     ∇
```

5.8   Important points

Communicaton with the terminal: □ and ⍞.

Functions: ⍏ T ⊥ ⍒ ⍋ ⍎ ∈ ;.

Comment: ⍝.

6.1 Local and global variables

Let us write a function that can trace a histogram†

```
    ∇ SCA HIST V
[1]    I←⌈/V←⌊.5+V÷SCA
[2]    L:' ⎕'[1+I≤V]
[3]    →(0<I←I-1)/L
    ∇
```

with V as the right hand argument: a numerical vector whose histogram is to be traced; and SCA as the left hand argument: a numerical scalar – this is the scale factor.

Line 1: gives the elements of V divided by the scale (rounded up to the nearest whole number) and calculates in I the maximum height of the histogram.

Line 2: prints a space or a 'quad' after comparing the current value of I to the values of V.

Line 3: loops onto line 2 having subtracted 1 from I; the function ends when I is zero.

```
    )VARS
```

Let us ask for the list of variables: there are none. Let us start the execution, then ask for the list of variables again:

```
      1 HIST 1 2 3 4 2 3 1
       ⎕
     ⎕⎕ ⎕
   ⎕⎕⎕⎕⎕
  ⎕⎕⎕⎕⎕⎕⎕
      )VARS
I
        I

0
```

---

† The reader might find it helpful to consult section 4.3(*c*) where an alternative way of writing this function is given.

I was created at the time of execution of the function HIST, but on the other hand, there is no trace of the variables SCA, V, and L.

It would be interesting to stop the function HIST while it is being executed to find out what has happened to these last three variables. To do this we use the system function □SS (see section 3.8):

```
      3  □SS 'HIST'
3
```

Remember that this operation enables us to interrupt the execution of HIST before line 3. Let us recommence execution of HIST

```
      1 HIST 1 2 3 4 3 1
   □
HIST[3] *
```

As expected the execution is interrupted at line 3. Let us ask for the list of variables.

```
      )VARS
I        L        SCA      V
```

We see now that SCA, V and L still exist; their values are:

```
      SCA
1
      I
4

      L
2
      V
1  2  3  4  3  1
```

Let us cancel out the interruption on line 3:

```
      3  □RS 'HIST'
3
```

and resume execution.

```
         →3
   □□□
  □□□□
□□□□□□
      )VARS
I
```

A new)VARS command only supplies us with I.

We can see from this example that two sorts of variable exist:

   those that remain (I),

   those that disappear after HIST has been executed (V, SCA, L).

These last three variables only exist within the function HIST where they have been defined, they are said to be *variables local to* HIST. On the other hand, I, although defined in HIST exists outside this function, and is called a *global variable.*

We note from this example that arguments and labels are always variables local to the function in which they are defined.

More generally, in APL variables can be declared as being local to a function by writing each variable, preceded by ';' after the function heading on the same line. Let us make variable I local to HIST, since it is only useful to us in this function.

```
      ∇HIST[0□0]
[0]   SCA HIST V;I
[1]   [□]
    ∇ SCA HIST V;I
[1]   I←⌈/V←⌊.5+V÷SCA
[2]   L:' □'[1+I≤V]
[3]   →(0<I←I-1)/L
    ∇
[4]   ∇
```

Returning to our previous example, we erase the variable I and restart execution:

```
      )ERASE I

    1 HIST 1 2 3 4 3 1
      □
     □□□
    □□□□
 □□□□□□
      )VARS
```

The command)VARS no longer gives us anything; the variable I has become a local variable.

6.2 Static block structure

The program structure in APL, called *static block structure*, is linked to the definition of the identifiers (variables, labels, functions).

For any APL function we differentiate between two static blocks:

the active workspace (WS: WORKSPACE);
the local variables (arguments, labels and others) of the function.

Let us return to the example of the histogram and imagine that we have defined a new function FF:

```
    ∇ FF V
[1]   I←⌈/V←⌊.5+V
    ∇
```

Representation of the different blocks and the different variables is given in Figure 7. Different functions can have local variables with the same name. This block structure is valid in all workspaces. All the identifiers defined in a workspace are unknown outside that space.

6.3   Dynamism of local variables

Let us define a variable I for which we specify a value,

```
I←ι10
I
1   2   3   4   5   6   7   8   9   10
```

Figure 7

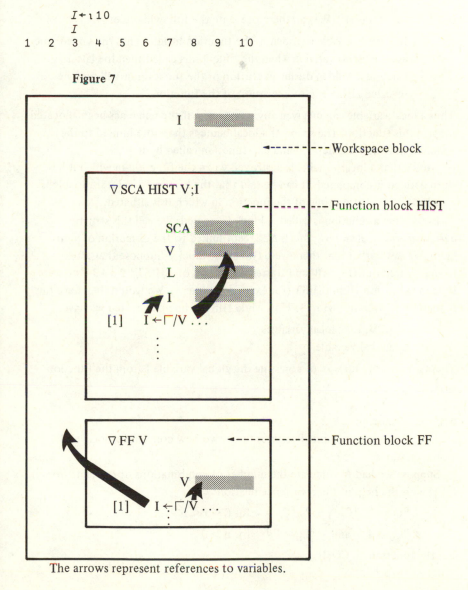

The arrows represent references to variables.

then ask for a new execution of HIST to see if the value of I has been modified.

```
        1 HIST 1 1 2 4 3 1
     □
     □□
     □□□
□□□□□□
        I
1   2   3   4   5   6   7   8   9   10
```

No, I still contains ι10. We can therefore state the following rule:

> If a local variable (defined in the function heading) has the same name as an existing variable when the function is called then the latter variable is hidden during execution of the function; it will only be revealed at the end of execution of the function.

Thus a local variable can be given any name, even if the name has been allocated outside this function. The scope of a local name is therefore limited to the function in which it is defined and any function called by it.

Notice that a local variable is destroyed when the function in which it has been defined is completed. It can be said that the lifetime of a local variable is equal to the execution time of the function in which it is situated.

Every time a function is called, a block is created. We call this structure a *dynamic block structure*; this is a concept linked to the execution of a program. We saw earlier that there were two static blocks. Suppose that after having carried out G ← 'AB' and started execution of 1 HIST 1 2 3 4 3 1 we were to stop execution within HIST (for example at line 3). We would then have the organisation given in Figure 8. Thus while HIST is being executed we have:

> SCA, V, I, L: local variables,
> G: global variable.

There is therefore no way of accessing the global variable I from the function HIST.

6.4   Recursion

A further example illustrates these two new concepts of local and global variables.

Suppose we had to calculate the number of combinations of r objects from n (^nC_r) with the help of the recurrence relation:

$$^nC_r = {}^{n-1}C_{r-1} + {}^{n-1}C_r \quad \Big\} \quad \text{for } 0 < r < n$$
$$^nC_0 = 1 \quad \text{and} \quad {}^nC_n = 1 \quad \text{for } n > 0$$

Let the function be COMP:

```
      ∇COMP[□]∇
   ∇ Z←N COMP R
[1]    Z←1
[2]    →((R=N)∨(R=0))/0
[3]    A←N-1
[4]    Z←(A COMP R-1)+A COMP R
   ∇
```

Line 2: allows an exit from the function if N = R or R = 0 after putting Z
(the result) equal to 1.

Line 3: assigns the value N−1 to A.

Line 4: specifies the result Z by calling COMP twice, once with the arguments
A and R−1, and once with A and R. Let us try out our function to calculate
$^4C_2$.

```
      4 COMP 2
4
      2!4
6
```

Figure 8

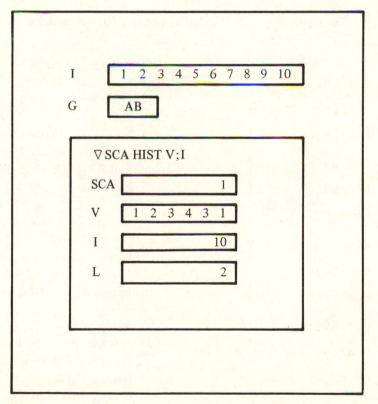

Unfortunately it gives 4 as the result, but everyone knows that $^4C_2 = 6$. This can be verified using the dyadic function ! derived from the characters ' and . $R\,!\,N = {}^NC_R$. To find out where the error lies, we shall examine in more detail the path followed by the APL interpreter in its execution of the function COMP.

Let us first of all represent the sequence of calls of COMP by a diagram, Figure 9, taking care to number them chronologically. Now let us request a trace of execution of the function:

```
      2  3  4  □ST  'COMP'
2    3    4
```

On the trace, we shall see:

Line 2: $\rightarrow$ passage in sequence (the test is false);

$\qquad \rightarrow 0$ exit from the function (the test is true) $Z=1$;

Line 3: the value of A (this is a global variable and therefore only the last value is to be considered);

Line 4: the value of Z when the function is exited outside the test on the first line.

The sequence of calls of COMP is numbered in chronological order.

			Entry into 4 COMP 2	
$COMP[2]\rightarrow$		$A = 3$	1 Entry into 3 COMP 2	
$COMP[3]$ 2			2 Entry into 2 COMP 2	
		$A = 2$	Exit for $N = R$	$Z = 1$
$COMP[2]\rightarrow0$	}2		3 Entry into 2 COMP 1	
			4 Entry into 1 COMP 1	
$COMP[2]\rightarrow$		$A = 1$	Exit for $N = R$	$Z = 1$
$COMP[3]$ 1			5 Entry into 1 COMP 0	
			Exit for $R = 0$	$Z = 1$
$COMP[2]\rightarrow0$ }4			We can now evaluate 2 COMP 1	
$COMP[2]\rightarrow0$ }5			$Z = 1 + 1 = 2$	
$COMP[4]$ 2			We can now evaluate 3 COMP 2	
			$Z = 2 + 1 = 3$	
$COMP[4]$ 3			6 Entry into 3 COMP 1	
$COMP[2]\rightarrow0$	}6		Exit is on line 1, therefore	
$COMP[4]$ 4			$N = R$ or $R = 0$. We have just	
			called A COMP R−1, the	
4			last value of A being 1;	
			hence the problem.	

Trace of the function

(braces grouping: }3 }1, }2)

We have just called 1 COMP 1 and not 3 COMP 1 and this is where the error lies; A should have had the value of 3. If, on the other hand, we had made this variable local, every time COMP was called, the values of A would have been hidden in order to be reinstated at 'the correct moment'. Representing the successive calls for COMP with a dynamic block structure allows us to visualise this phenomenon better; every time it is called we create a block containing the variables used (see Figure 10). The scope of the names is well illustrated by such a figure.

Let us make the variable A local:

```
        ∇COMP[0□0]
[0]     Z←N COMP R;A∇

        □RT 'COMP'
0   1   2   3   4
        4 COMP 2
6
        ∇COMP[□]∇
    ∇ Z←N COMP R;A
[1]     Z←1
[2]     →((R=N)∨(R=0))/0
[3]     A←N-1
[4]     Z←(A COMP R-1)+A COMP R
    ∇
```

The function is now correct.

We have just written a *recursive* function. A function is said to be recursive if it is called directly (simple recursion) or via other functions (crossed recursion).

6.5   Static and dynamic structure

Consider a function A which can activate the chain of calls given in Figure 11. Suppose that the function is as illustrated in Figure 12. The dynamic

Figure 9

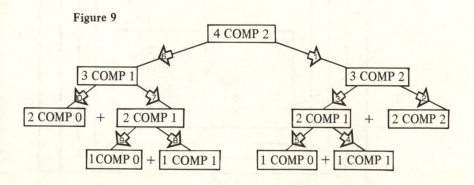

Figure 10

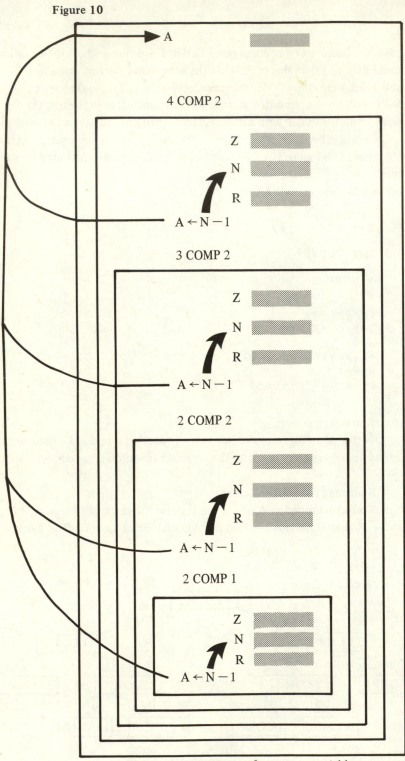

The arrows represent references to variables.

Figure 11

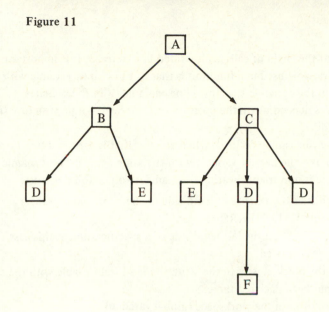

Figure 12

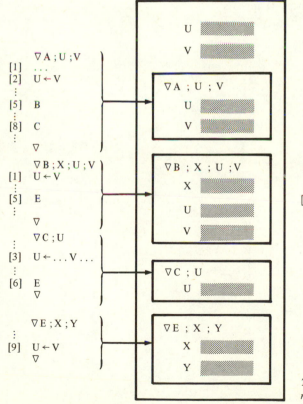

```
        ∇A ; U ; V
[1]     ...
[2]     U ← V
⋮
[5]     B
⋮
[8]     C
        ∇
```

```
        ∇B ; X ; U ; V
[1]     U ← V
⋮
[5]     E
        ∇
```

```
        ∇C ; U
⋮
[3]     U ← ... V ...
⋮
[6]     E
        ∇
```

```
        ∇E ; X ; Y
⋮
[9]     U ← V
        ∇
```

```
            U
            V

        ∇A ; U ; V
            U
            V

        ∇B ; X ; U ; V
            X
            U
            V

        ∇C ; U
            U

        ∇E ; X ; Y
            X
            Y
```

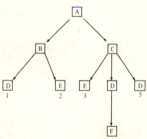

The numbers 1, 2 ... 5
represent the routes

representation of the chain of calls is illustrated in Figure 13. It is important to notice that the variable used in a function is that of the nearest variable with the same name in the dynamic structure. For example, V in E designates different variables depending on the position of E in the dynamic structure (see Figure 14).

The following rule can be defined: when an identifier is used in a function, the APL system uses the nearest variable with the same name in the dynamic structure. If there is no variable bearing this name, two possibilities exist:

(1)   the identifier is on the right hand side of the expression; in this case it is an error: VALUE ERROR;

(2)   the identifier is on the left hand side of a specification; in this case a variable is created:

(*a*) in the block closest to the structure if a local variable with the same name has been declared there;

(*b*) otherwise in the workspace (global variable).

In practice, the number of dynamic blocks has a limit, which is governed by the resources of the machine (the memory) and the number of variables. If this limit is reached, an error message appears:

WS FULL

Let us try it:

```
     ∇ FF A;U;V
[1]    U←A
[2]    V←2,(ρA)ρA
[3]    FF A,A
     ∇

     FF 1
WS FULL
FF[2] V←2,(ρA)ρA
     ∧
     )SINL
```

FF[2]	A	U	V
FF[3]	A	U	V
FF[3]	A	U	V
FF[3]	A	U	V
FF[3]	A	U	V
FF[3]	A	U	V
FF[3]	A	U	V
FF[3]	A	U	V
FF[3]	A	U	V
FF[3]	A	U	V
FF[3]	A	U	V
FF[3]	A	U	V
FF[3]	A	U	V
FF[3]	A	U	V

Figure 13

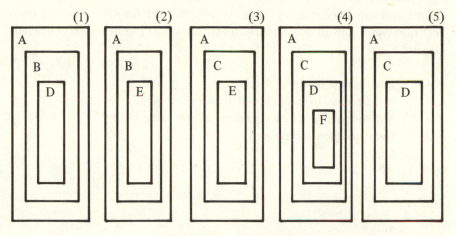

Figure 14

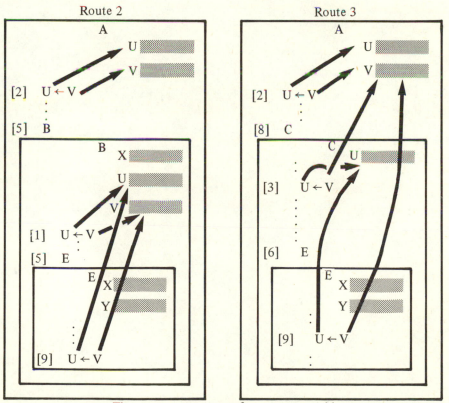

The arrows represent references to variables.

It should be noted that an image of the structure of the dynamic block can be obtained with the command)SINL. It gives, for each function appearing in the interrupt vector, the list of local variables (in certain APL systems this command is called SIV).

6.6   Important points

The structure of variables is that of a *static block*;

The structure of execution is that of a *dynamic block*;

Local and global variables;

Recursions;

)SINL.

We shall now try to reinforce what we have learnt in the previous chapters by writing a small, deliberately simple, application. This will allow us to introduce new concepts (system or primitive functions, commands ...) which, to prevent the text from becoming turgid, will not be described in detail, but rather introduced as an integral part of the application. The aim of this chapter is, in fact, to show that an APL system offers more extensive facilities than we have considered so far.

Suppose we want to do a simplified costing of the sales of one or more types of product. Each month, we have to record, for each class of product, the number of sales, the unit price and the turnover (obtained by multiplying these first two items of data).

We could solve this problem with what we have learnt so far, using variables, but that would lack flexibility in managing several types of product. We are therefore going to introduce a new way of arranging data: files.

Numerous APL systems offer this facility in different forms, one of the most widely used being APL*PLUS of the STSC which we shall use here. This system considers an APL file as a collection of data or components referenced by a number. The components can be an array of any rank or type. Before any file is used, it must be created with the function □FCREATE:

        'SALES' □*FCREATE* 3

We have thus created the file SALES which we shall designate henceforth by its number, 3, arbitrarily chosen, for the duration of the working session.

Let us return to our application: in the file, the first component will be the list of product names, the second the current unit prices, updated every month if necessary. Each of the subsequent components will represent the monthly sales in the form of a matrix, one row containing the number of articles sold, the unit price and finally the turnover of the product in question.

Let NAMESPRODUCTS be the matrix of the product names (formed by the function WORDS of chapter 5, for example). We create the first component of the file with:

> *NAMESPRODUCTS* *□FAPPEND* 3

The function □FAPPEND adds a component to the end of the file 3 (which, until now, did not contain any); we have thus entered the first component. If the vector PRICE contains the unit prices, we create the second component with:

> *PRICE* *□FAPPEND* 3

When a file is no longer in use, this must be indicated to the APL system with:

> *□FUNTIE* 3

We have just 'closed' or 'untied' the file, which will be preserved in the same state in which it was created for subsequent use. To use it again, all we have to do is type:

> *'SALES'* *□FTIE* 1

In this way we 'open' or 'tie' the SALES file, this time under the number 1.

Let us write the main function for the problem. First of all the computer asks what file the user wants to work on and it opens under the number 1:

```
     ∇  UPD;I
[1]     ▯←'WHAT FILE DO YOU WISH TO UPDATE ? '
[2]     ▯□FTIE 1
[3]    FLIM←□FLIM 1
```

The function □FLIM gives a vector of two elements containing the numbers of the first existing component and the first free component. The first existing component does not necessarily come under the number 1: a number is assigned definitively to a component at the time of its creation. The function □FDROP destroys components at the beginning or the end of a file; this function has a left operand analagous to that of the function ↓ to identify the components to be destroyed.

Let us assign the variables PRODUCTS and UNITP with the names and current unit prices of the products:

```
[4]    PRODUCTS←□FREAD 1 1
[5]    UNITP←□FREAD 1 2
```

Next we determine the month to be recorded taking into account the size of the file:

```
[6]    NEXTM←¯2+FLIM[2]
[7]    NPROD←(ι0)ρρPRODUCTS
```

NPROD is a scalar giving the number of products.

We want to test the consistency of the input data by comparing it to the sales of previous months. For this we are going to construct a matrix **REF** containing the sales figures for no more than the last three months, and for January we shall use a special matrix:

```
[8]    REF←(NPROD,2)ρ¯1 1×100000
[9]    →(NEXTM=1)/END
[10]   I←1+NEXTM
[11]   REF←(NPROD,0)ρ0
[12] LP:→(I=2)/END
[13]   →(3=1↓ρREF)/END
[14]   REF←REF,(□FREAD 1,I)[;1]
[15]   I←I-1
[16]   →LP
```

For the other months we read the components one by one beginning with the last, and stopping either when the matrix **REF** has 3 columns, or when all the existing monthly components have been read.

All that remains is to create a matrix containing the names of the months:

```
[17] END:MONTH←'JANUARY
                  FEBRUARY      MARCH        APRIL
[18]   MONTH←MONTH,'MAY
                  JUNE          JULY         AUGUST
[19]   MONTH←MONTH,'SEPTEMBER
                  OCTOBER       NOVEMBER     DECEMBER
[20]   MONTH←12 12ρMONTH
```

Finally the function is completed by suggesting a 'menu' giving the possible uses and the names of the corresponding functions:

```
[21]   'TO INTRODUCE A NEW MONTH : ENTRY'
[22]   'TO PRINT                 : EDIT'
[23]   'TO END THE SESSION       : END'
       ∇
[24]   ∇
```

Let us now write the function **ENTRY**:

```
    ∇ ENTRY;NUMP;EAM;L;R;RR;PRT;PN
[1]    'INTRODUCTION OF SALES OF ',,MONTH[NEXTM;]
[2]    EAM←ι0
[3]    NUMP←1
```

A message indicates to the user what month he is going to record. EAM will contain the sales figures and NUMP will be used to manage the data aquisition loop.

```
[4]  INP:PN←PRT←UNITP[NUMP]
[5]    R←¯1
[6]    MEANREF←MEAN J←REF[NUMP;]
[7]    DEVREF←2×DEV J
```

PN and PRT are initialised with the current unit price of the product in question, R will contain the sales figures. MEANREF and DEVREF represent the mean and twice the mean of the standard deviation of the reference sales: these values are calculated with the functions MEAN and DEV.

```
[8]   LP:RR←('-',PRODUCTS[NUMP;],'
                  (UNITPRICE : ',(▼PRT),')? ')IENT 0 2
```

The function IENT displays the message given in the left hand argument – the name and the unit price of the product – and requests an input which should be 0, 1, or 2 numerical integer values (in order to simplify the operation we are using integers to represent the prices). The result RR is thus an empty vector (if the user just confirms the previous entry) or a vector of one or two elements, depending on whether the user has just indicated the number of articles sold, or also modified the unit price.

```
[9]    →((0=ρRR)∧R≥0)/ENDB
[10]   PN←¯1↑RR←2↑RR,PRT
```

If RR is empty and R has already been defined (request for confirmation) we can pass to the end of the loop. If not, RR is restructured so that it is always two elements in size, PN taking the value of the second element.

```
[11]   →(.15≥(|PN-PRT)÷PRT)/PNOK
[12]   'PRICE VARIATION OF MORE THAN 15 PER 100,
                      PRESS RETURN OR RETYPE.'
[13]   →LP
[14]   PNOK:PRT←PN
```

We verify that the unit price does not vary more than 15%. If not we request confirmation. PN is updated and we verify the sales figures (first element of RR):

```
[15]   →(DEVREF≥|MEANREF-R←1↑RR)/ENDB
[16]   'MEAN : ',(▼⌊.5+MEANREF),'.PRESS RETURN OR RETYPE.'
[17]   →LP
```

and request confirmation if this figure differs more than twice the standard deviation from the reference mean.

When all this is correct, we record the new price and the number of sales:

```
[18]   ENDB:UNITP[NUMP]←PN
[19]   EAM←EAM,R
```

and we go on to the next product:

```
[20]   →(NPROD≥NUMP←NUMP+1)/INP
```

Once all the products have been reviewed, we transform the vectors EAM and UNITP to a single matrix:

```
[21]   EAM+EAM,[1.5]UNITP
```

For this we use a special form of the function ',' called 'laminate', where a decimal value for the index indicates that a new dimension has been created, in this case, after the first dimension: the two vectors thus become single column matrices before being joined together into one matrix of two columns. Then we add a third column, which is the product of the first two, and we write the result at the end of the file:

```
[22]   EAM+EAM,×/EAM
[23]   EAM □FAPPEND 1
```

Finally, we update the unit prices with the function □FREPLACE which allows the specified component to be replaced:

```
[24]   UNITP □FREPLACE 1 2
```

and we offer the user the opportunity to obtain the listing of the recorded month:

```
[25]   □←'DO YOU WANT A LIST (Y/N) ? '
[26]   →0×ι'N'=1↑□
[27]   LIST NEXTM
     ∇
```

The EDIT function is simply:

```
     ∇ EDIT
[1]    LIST ι12
     ∇
```

and it is left to the function LIST to verify the months that are actually recorded. This function will only edit the turnover with the totals by product and by month.

```
     ∇ LIST NBM;M;SEP;I
[1]    NBM←(NBM≤⁻3+1↓□FLIM 1)/NBM←,NBM
[2]    M←(NPROD,0)ρ0
```

The parameter NBM contains the numbers of the months to be edited; we delete from this list those that are not recorded and we initialise M, a matrix that will contain the set of turnover figures to be edited.

Let us write the heading of the listing:

```
[3]    SEP←ρ□←'PRODUCTS              ',(,MONTH[NBM;]),'TOTALS'
[4]    SEPρ'+'
```

A loop allows us to read the monthly information and to add it to the matrix M:

```
[5]    NBM←NBM+2
[6]    L1:M←M,(□FREAD 1,1ρNBM)[;3]
[7]    →(0≠ρNBM←1↓NBM)/L1
```

All that we need do now is create a column containing the totals by product, and to print the whole program:

```
[8]    M←M,+/M
[9]    PRODUCTS,0 4↓12 0⍕M
[10]   SEPρ'-'
```

The function ⍕ used in its dyadic form, allows us to specify the characteristics needed for editing: the first figure, 12, gives the field width, while the second indicates the number of decimal places, in this case 0 since we are editing integers (a complete description of this function is beyond the scope of this book).

Finally we add a line giving the monthly totals:

```
[11]   'TOTALS          ',4↓12 0⍕+/M
[12]   SEPρ'+'
```

All that remains is for the functions DEV, MEAN, END and IENT to be written. The function END will close the file and destroy all the superfluous variables, in this case all the variables created by the principal function UPD:

```
    ∇ END ;I
[1]   □FUNTIE 1
[2]   I←□EX □NL 2
    ∇
```

For this we use two new system functions, □EX and □NL. The function □NL takes as its argument an integer vector whose elements can, in particular, equal 2 or 3. The result is a character matrix containing the names of the variables (if 2 appears in the argument) and/or the functions (if 3 appears in the argument) of the workspace. There is an inverse function; □NC, whose argument is a name or a name matrix, and whose result is a vector indicating the nature of the corresponding APL object:

```
      □NC 'UPD
3
      □NC 'PRODUCTS'
2
      □NC 2 6ρ'UNITP ENTRY '
2   3
```

The function □EX also takes a name matrix as its argument, and destroys, whenever possible, the corresponding objects, whether variables or functions. Its result is a logic vector that indicates whether the object has been destroyed (1) or not (0); in this way it is impossible to destroy a label, or pendant, or suspended, functions.

It is unnecessary to create and program the functions MEAN, DEV and IENT every time they are used; rather, we shall copy them into our workspace from an inactive (or saved) space with the command)COPY:

```
)COPY 10 STATS MEAN DEV
```

In contrast to the command)LOAD which replaces the active workspace with a copy of the workspace indicated, the command)COPY only adds specified objects, here the functions MEAN and DEV which it finds in the STATS workspace of user 10. However if the names MEAN and DEV already corresponded to variables or functions, the latter would be destroyed and replaced by the objects copied. There is a variation of the command)COPY which allows existing objects to be protected. This is the command)PCOPY. It indicates the names of the objects that have not been copied:

```
)PCOPY 10 STATS MEAN
NOT COPIED : MEAN
```

This is especially useful when a complete workspace is being copied, since only the identification of the workspace is given, and not a list of names:

```
)COPY 10 STATS
```

or better still:

```
)PCOPY 10 STATS
```

Let us recover the IENT function:

```
)COPY 11 CONV IENT
```

Our workspace is now complete and we can save it (see chapter 2). Prior to this we shall introduce the system variable □LX which is the 'latent expression', that is to say an expression that is automatically executed by the APL system at the time of loading a workspace. As a rule this variable is empty:

```
ρ□LX
```
0

In this example we would like the function UPD to be executed automatically, we therefore write:

```
□LX←'UPD'
```

then:

```
)SAVE COMPTA
```

Note that this command gives the workspace the name COMPTA, which we can verify with the command)WSID:

```
      )WSID
IS COMPTA
```

A copy is then made and given the same name. The command)LIB lists the names of the user's inactive workspaces:

```
      )LIB
COMPTA
```

In addition the command)WSID allows the name of the active workspace to be changed:

```
      )WSID UPDF
WAS COMPTA
```

Notice, while on the subject, that there is some protection in the command)SAVE:

```
      )SAVE COMPTA
NOT SAVED, THIS WS IS UPDF
```

In fact, when the workspace indicated already exists the old version is replaced by the new one – checking the identification of the workspace means that we can avoid inadvertently destroying an inactive one.

Now let us try out our application:

```
      )LOAD COMPTA
  SAVED    83/03/21   12.42.43
WHAT FILE DO YOU WISH TO UPDATE ? SALES
TO INTRODUCE A NEW MONTH : ENTRY
TO PRINT                 : EDIT
TO END THE SESSION       : END
```

The function UPD has certainly been executed and we have indicated that we want to update the file SALES. Now we can set the function ENTRY into action:

```
      ENTRY
INTRODUCTION OF SALES OF JANUARY
-MIXERS          (UNITPRICE : 155  )? 25
-KNIVES          (UNITPRICE : 225  )? 35
-SPITS           (UNITPRICE : 100  )? 22
-DRILLS          (UNITPRICE : 100  )? 12
-SANDERS         (UNITPRICE : 120  )? 10
-VENTILATORS     (UNITPRICE : 100  )? 7
-GYROSCOPES      (UNITPRICE : 250  )? 3
-FIRE ALARMS     (UNITPRICE : 300  )? 56
-RUBBER STAMPS   (UNITPRICE : 175  )? 9
DO YOU WANT A LIST (Y/N) ? Y
PRODUCTS         JANUARY      TOTALS
++++++++++++++++++++++++++++++++++++++
```

```
MIXERS              3875          3875
KNIVES              7875          7875
SPITS               2200          2200
DRILLS              1200          1200
SANDERS             1200          1200
VENTILATORS          700           700
GYROSCOPES           750           750
FIRE ALARMS        16800         16800
RUBBER STAMPS       1575          1575
- - - - - - - - - - - - - - - - - - - - - - - - - - - -
TOTALS             36175         36175
+++++++++++++++++++++++++++++++++++++++++
```

This example is still in its basic form. One of the first improvements that could be made would be to transform the function UPD to a main function which would itself call the other functions at the request of the user. This would permit all the global variables to be made local to UPD and would guide the user better.

We have only given a glimpse of the possibilities of a file system using APL. In this field, as with any language, there is much left for you to discover and experiment with.

Important points
Primitive functions:

Format: ⊤
Laminate: ,

Commands

)COPY   )PCOPY
)SAVE
)LOAD
)LIB
)WSID

System functions:

□EX □NC □NL
□FCREATE □FTIE □FUNTIE □FAPPEND □FREPLACE
□FDROP □FREAD.

EXERCISES

CHAPTER 1

1. Give two monadic functions which, when applied to 1.78, give 1.

2. What reply does the APL system give to the following expressions:
   - (a) $-\bar{3}$
   - (b) $\bar{}-3$
   - (c) $--3$
   - (d) $\bar{}\bar{3}$

3. Work out:
   - (a) $\bar{7}\lceil 4$
   - (b) $-7\lceil 4$

4. Are the following expressions correct?
   - (a) $1.25E\bar{1}2$
   - (b) $1.25E-12$
   - (c) $1.25E12$
   - (d) $1.25 \times E12$
   - (e) $1.25E1+2$

5. During a work session, a user types in the expressions:
   1. $A \leftarrow 3$
   2. $B \leftarrow \bar{2}$
   3. $A \leftarrow B * A$
   4. $B \leftarrow \times B$
   5. $B \leftarrow B \lceil A$

   What are the values associated with the variables A and B after execution of the last instruction, when the order in which they are typed in is:
   - (a) 1-2-3-4-5
   - (b) 1-2-4-3-5
   - (c) 1-2-5-4-3
   - (d) 2-4-3-1-5

CHAPTER 2

1. Give two monadic functions which, when applied to 0, give 1.

2. Which of the following expressions are incorrect?
   (a) $X \leftarrow \times 3$
   (b) $X \leftarrow 3 \times$
   (c) $X \leftarrow 5A \div B + C$
   (d) $X \leftarrow (A \div B + C$

3. If the evaluation of the following expressions give the results in brackets, what must the value of the variable A be?
   (a) $2 + A \times 3 + 5$ (162)
   (b) $2 + (A \times 3) + 5$ (67)
   (c) $10 + 6 \times 4 + A \times 2$ (130)
   (d) $10 + (6 \times 4) + A \times 2$ (130)

4. Does the APL expression $(X*2) - (2 \times X \times Y) + Y*2$ correspond to the expansion $(x-y)^2$? If not, correct it.

5. Which of the following APL expressions give the discriminant of a quadratic equation with the coefficients A, B and C?
   (a) $(B*2) - 4 \times A \times C$
   (b) $(B*2) - (4 \times A \times C)$
   (c) $B*2 - 4 \times A \times C$
   (d) $(B \times B) - 4 \times A \times C$
   (e) $B \times B - 4 \times A \times C$

6. Rewrite the following expressions deleting the redundant brackets:
   1. $5 \times ((100 \div (+/(\iota 20)))) - 6$
   2. $(+/(! \lceil *(\iota 3)) - 1) + 50$
   (a) without modifying the order of the operands;
   (b) modifying the order of the operands.

7. In order to calculate its sum total of monthly bills, a finance company uses the following formula:

   $$P = Ai \; \frac{(1+i)^n}{(1+i)^n - 1}$$

   where:
   P = sum total of bills;
   A = capital borrowed;
   i = monthly rate of interest;
   n = number of monthly instalments.
   Write the corresponding APL expression.

8. Work out $1 = 1 \times 1 < 1 \leqslant 1 \geqslant 1 > 1$.

9. Give more concise expressions for the following:
   (a) $(A \times B) \wedge A \geqslant B$
   (b) $(A = B) \vee A < B$
   (c) $(A \times B) \vee A \geqslant B$

10. TEXT is a character vector. Write an APL expression that gives 1 when the proposition is verified and 0 if not:
    (a) the letter X appears exactly three times in TEXT
    (b) the letter X appears at least once in TEXT
    (c) all the letters in TEXT are Xs.

11. (a) Write an expression that assigns the value 10 to X if $Y < Z$ and the value 2 if $Y > Z$.
    (b) Write an expression that will assign the value 5 to X if $Y = Z$, the value 2 if $Y < Z$ and the value 8 if $Y > Z$.

12. Write an expression that gives the number of the quadrant in which the point with the coordinates (x, y) lies.

13. x and y are two vectors representing the coordinates of two points A and B. Write expressions giving the distance between these two points:
    (a) $d(A, B) = \Sigma (x_i - y_i)^2)^{1/2}$
    (b) $d(A, B) = (\Sigma |x_i - y_i|^P)^{1/p}$
    (c) $d(A, B) = \underset{i}{MAX} |x_i - y_i|$

14. Let R be a vector of dimension n. The arithmetic, geometric and harmonic mean of the elements of R are given by:

$$A = \frac{\Sigma r_i}{n}$$

$$B = (\Pi r_i)^{1/n}$$

$$C = \frac{n}{\Sigma \frac{1}{r_i}}$$

Write the corresponding APL expressions.

15. Calculate e^x by summation of its series expansion to the order n:

$$e^x = \sum_{i=0}^{n} \frac{x^i}{i!}$$

CHAPTER 3

1. What is the name of the function defined by the following headings?
    (*a*) ∇ *ONE TWO*
    (*b*) ∇ *ONE ← TWO THREE FOUR*
    (*c*) ∇ *ONE ← TWO THREE*
    (*d*) ∇ *ONE TWO ← THREE FOUR*
    (*e*) ∇ *ONE ← TWO*
    (*f*) ∇ *ONE*
    (*g*) ∇ *ONE TWO THREE*

2. What is the number of the next line executed for the values of the variables indicated?
    (*a*) $[3] \rightarrow 0 \times \iota N \geqslant 38$ (N=10)
    (*b*) $[5] \rightarrow 2 \times \iota I = 17$ (I=17)
    (*c*) $[8] \rightarrow 0 \times \iota 8 \geqslant \rho T$ (T=6 2 4 1)
    (*d*) $[3] \rightarrow 2 + 5 \times I = 5$ (I=5)
    (*e*) $[6] \rightarrow 2 - I \div 2$ (I=3)

3. Write branchings for the following:
    (*a*) exit from the function during execution if all the elements of the vector W are greater than 87, otherwise, continue in sequence;
    (*b*) go to line 11 if the vector TEXT contains the letter Z, if not go to line 27;
    (*c*) TAB is an object of rank less than or equal to 2. Exit from the function during execution if TAB is a scalar, continue in sequence if TAB is a vector, go to line 17 if TAB is a matrix.

4. A user writes a function to work out the scalar product of two vectors $\vec{A}$ and $\vec{B}$:

$$\vec{A} \cdot \vec{B} = \sum_{i} a_i b_i$$

He defines it thus:

```
    ∇ A PRODUCT B
[1]   +/A×B
    ∇
```

(*a*) To work out the scalar product of the vectors ‾1 2 and 6 4, he requests the following:
(*a1*) (‾1 2) *PRODUCT* 6 4
(*a2*) (‾1 2) *PRODUCT* (6 4)
(*a3*) ‾1 2 *PRODUCT* 6 4
(*a4*) (−1 2) *PRODUCT* 6 4
Does he obtain the anticipated result?

(*b*) Now he needs to calculate the angle between the two vectors. The formula that he uses is:

$$\cos \alpha = \frac{\vec{A} \cdot \vec{B}}{[(\vec{A} \cdot \vec{A}) \times (\vec{B} \cdot \vec{B})]^{1/2}}$$

Write a function ∇ X ANGLE Y which uses the function **PRODUCT** as defined above and which supplies the cosine of the angle between the two vectors X and Y.

(*c*) Having written the function ANGLE, he wants to calculate the cosine of the angle between the vectors ⁻1 2 and 6 4.

(*c1*) How must he formulate his instruction?

(*c2*) The interpreter's reply is a **SYNTAX ERROR** situated in the first call of **PRODUCT** by ANGLE. Why?

(*d*) To correct this error, he changes the heading of the function **PRODUCT**, which then has the following form:

```
     ∇  R←A PRODUCT B
[1]     R←+/A×B
     ∇
```

(*d1*) To test the new version of his function, he types in:
⁻1 2 **PRODUCT** 6 4. The interpreter does indeed supply the result, but along with a **VALUE ERROR** message. Why?

(*d2*) Remove this error by correcting **PRODUCT**.

(*d3*) With this last version of **PRODUCT**, does ANGLE function correctly?

5. During a working session, a user types in commands and obtains the following replies:

```
      )VARS
SELLPRICE   COSTPRICE   QUANTITY
      )FNS
PROFIT
      )SI
PROFIT[3] ★
```

(*a*) What is the meaning of this information?

(*b*) To resume execution of **PROFIT**, different solutions are considered:

(*b1*) →0

(*b2*) →ι0

(*b3*) →3

(*b4*) →6357

What happens with each of these commands?

(*c*) On typing in →3, the system replies:

PROFIT[3] ★

Give an explanation for this response. How can it be erased?

(*d*) Having made the preceding correction, the user types in →3 again. Ten minutes later, he still has had no reply from the computer. Help him.

(*e*) The variable SELLPRICE is calculated from a unit price and the variable QUANTITY. So that this will be calculated automatically, the user defines a function heading:

∇ *R←UNITPRICE SELLPRICE QUANTITY*

The system replies with **DEFN ERROR**. Why? What solutions can you suggest?

6. Write a function that calculates the bonus for a car insurance.

∇*R←INSRATE BONUS PERIODS*

INSRATE : rate of insurance at the beginning of the period;
PERIODS : number of periods without claims;
      R : new rate of insurance.

The regulations for the calculation are as follows:

At the time of each annual renewal the premium due from the insured is determined by applying to the premium corresponding to the reference tariff of guaranteed risks an increase or decrease in the rate as shown in the following table:

Reduction (as a percentage)		Increase (as a percentage)	
After one annual period without claim	10	Claims arising in the annual period before expiry date:	
After two consecutive years without claim	10	One claim	10
		Two claims	40
Every additional annual period without claim gives a reduction of	5	Three claims	100
Total reduction cannot exceed	50	Any further claims arising during this period engender the additional increase of	100

Note – In derogation of the above provisions the rate of reduction per year without claim is uniformly 5% if the premium is less than or equal to 80% of the reference tariff of guaranteed risks at the time of renewal.
    The rate of reduction of 10% or 5%, or the rates of increase specified in the above table are applied as an increase or reduction to the rate at the time of the previous renewal.

7. Write a function to calculate the penalty for a car insurance.

   $\nabla R \leftarrow INSRATE\ PENALTY\ CLAIMS$

   R and **INSRATE** : same definitions as above;

             CLAIMS : number of claims during the period.

8. The relevant details of an insured person are contained in the variables:

       OLDTAX : rate of insurance at the beginning of the period;

     ACCIDENTS : number of claims made during the period;

        YEARS : number of years without claims at the beginning of the
   period.

   Write the function, headed ∇ **BONUSPENALTY** which uses this
   information and the functions defined above for:

   (*a*) determining the variable **YEARS**;

   (*b*) calculating the new rate of insurance **NEWRATE** for the insured
   person.

9. Suppose the function f(x) is to be integrated between the limits A and
   B.

   The area to be calculated is contained in a rectangle of height C, of
   breadth $B-A$, whose area is thus $S = C(B-A)$. The MONTE CARLO
   method consists of randomly generating N points uniformly distributed
   in the rectangle. The number of points M situated below the curve is
   counted. The integral is approximated by (M/N)S.

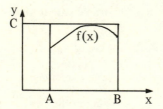

   Write a function ∇ A MONTECARLO B to carry out the integration.
   C should be taken as the maximum value of f for the abscissa generated,
   and the value 1000 for N.

10. Newton's method defined by the recurrence formulae:

    given x_0,

    $$x_{i+1} = x_i - \frac{f(x_i)}{f'(x_i)}$$

    converges on the solution of $f(x) = 0$ for a conveniently chosen value of
    x_0.

(*a*) Let ∇ R←F X be a function whose zero point we wish to find. Write a function ∇ R←DERIVE X supplying the value of the derivative of F at the point X using the formula:

$$f'(x) = \frac{f(x + 0.0001) - f(x)}{0.0001}$$

(*b*) Program Newton's method to calculate the zero point of f in the vicinity of x. The iteration should stop either when the absolute value of f at the discovered point is less than 0.0001, or when the number of iterations reaches a given value K.

∇ R←K NEWTON X

CHAPTER 4

1. Construct a matrix that will display the following figure at the terminal:

2. Write two different expressions to calculate the number of negative elements in a matrix M.

3. A, L and P are scalars equal to 1, 3 and 2 respectively. What do the following expressions give:
    (*a*) 1 2 3
    (*b*) 1,2,3,
    (*c*) A,P,L
    (*d*) APL
    (*e*) A P L
    (*f*) 'APL'

4. The area of a triangle can be calculated by the formula:

$$S = (P(P - A)(P - B)(P - C))^{1/2}$$

where P is the half-perimeter and A, B and C the lengths of the sides. Write an expression to perform this calculation; only one variable should be used, the vector SIDES, which contains the lengths of the three sides.

5. What is the result of applying ρρρ to a defined APL variable?

6. R is a numerical vector.
    (*a*) Select the integer elements of R;
    (*b*) Select the elements of R greater than its mean;
    (*c*) Select the largest of the elements of R less than its mean.

7. $A \leftarrow$, $B \leftarrow 4$.

    Are the objects A and B identical?

8. (*a*) Write a function $\nabla R \leftarrow$ SYMMETRY MAT, having as its argument a square matrix which gives 1 if it is symmetrical and 0 if not.

    (*b*) What happens when the argument is not a square matrix?

    (*c*) Modify your function such that the reply is 0 if the matrix is not square.

9. V is a numerical vector of dimension n. Find the vector W, of dimension $n-1$, such that:

$$w_i = \frac{v_i + v_{i+1}}{2}$$

10. (*a*) V is a numerical vector. Replace all the values of V less than 10 by 0.

    (*b*) TEXT is a character vector. Replace every X in TEXT by Z.

11. A is an integer scalar greater than 2. What do the following expressions give?

    (*a*) $\iota A[2]$

    (*b*) $\iota(,A)[2]$

    (*c*) $(\iota A)[2]$

12. (*a*) Write an expression to generate the identity matrix of dimension n,n.

    (*b*) Write an expression to generate the lower triangular matrix of dimension n,n whose elements that are not 0s are 1s.

    (*c*) Construct a matrix whose diagonal elements are equal to a given vector V.

    (*d*) Select the lower triangular matrix of a given matrix M.

13. M is a matrix. What are the differences between:

    (*a*) M[1;2]

    (*b*) M[,1;2]

    (*c*) M[1;,2]

    (*d*) M[,1;,2]

14. Write an expression that randomly selects an element of a matrix M.

15. Edit in the form of an array of n rows and 2 columns the sine and cosine of the angles from 0 to 2π in steps of $2\pi/n-1$.

    ∇ SINCOS N

    (See the definition of the monadic and dyadic operator $\circ$ at the end of the manual.)

16. Edit in the form of a lower triangular matrix Pascal's triangle of order n

    ∇ *PASCAL N*

    (See the definition of the dyadic operator ! at the end of the manual.)

17. DICTIONARY is a character matrix. Write a function giving 1 if the vector WORD is identical to one of the lines of the matrix and 0 if not.

    ∇ *WORD EXIST DICTIONARY*

18. List the prime numbers less than n. For this use Eratosthenes' sieve method: generate the series of n prime integers, then delete from this list all the multiples of 2 except 2; in the new list, delete all the multiples of 3 except 3, etc. . . .

    ∇ *R ← PRIME N*

    (See the definition of the dyadic operator | at the end of the manual.)

19. Convert a date written in roman characters to an integer.

    ∇ *ROMAN DATE*

    Remember that:
    M = 1000
    D = 500
    C = 100
    L = 50
    X = 10
    V = 5
    I = 1

20. You want to obtain the following array from the string of characters 'IVERSON':

    IVERSON
    VIVERSO
    EVIVERS
    REVIVER
    SREVIVE
    OSREVIV
    NOSREVI

    Write a function ∇ TRANSFORM CHAIN that edits the array corresponding to CHAIN.

CHAPTER 5

1. Write an expression that recognises a logic vector.

2. V is the vector 10 3 7 1; W is the vector 2 4 ¯1 3. What do the

following expressions give?

(a) $\square \leftarrow MAX \leftarrow \lceil/V$

(b) $MAX \leftarrow \square \leftarrow \lceil/V$

(c) $MAX \leftarrow \lceil/V \leftarrow \square$

(d) $MAX \leftarrow \lceil/V \leftarrow \boxdot$

(e) $1+\square \leftarrow MIN \leftarrow \lfloor/W$

(f) $1+\boxdot \leftarrow MIN \leftarrow \lfloor/W$

(g) $1+MIN \leftarrow \square+\lfloor/W$

(h) $1+MIN \leftarrow \boxdot+\lfloor/W$

3. Write a monadic function whose argument is an angle expressed in grads and which gives its value in degrees, minutes and seconds:

   ∇ *DEGREE* ← *CONVERTTO GRAD*

4. Write a monadic function whose argument is the vector of the values in degrees, minutes and seconds of an angle, and which gives its value in radians:

   ∇ *RADIAN* ← *CHANGETO DEGREE*

5. Write a function calculating the value of a polynomial at a point X:

   ∇ *R* ← *X POLYNOMIAL COEFFICIENT*

6. E1 and E2 are arrays of unknown structure, not necessarily identical, which contain unspecified elements of the same type.

   Write a function that gives the intersection of these two structures:

   ∇ *R* ← *E1 INTER E2*

7. With the same definitions for E1 and E2, write a function that combines these two structures:

   ∇ *R* ← *E1 UNION E2*

   (See the definition of the operator $\sim$ at the end of the manual.)

8. Write a conversational function that simulates cannon fire, headed ∇ CANNON.

   The function randomly selects the distance of a target between 1000 and 7500 m away, and informs the player of this distance; then it asks for the sight to be set (the angle that the cannon makes with the horizontal). The abscissa of the point of impact is calculated by the formula:

   x = 7500 sin 2α

   If the separation of the impact point of the shell and the target is greater than 50 m, its value is displayed and the player is asked to retire. Otherwise the shot is considered as successful and the player can, if he likes, attack another target. If the player does not wish to continue and gives a negative reply, the function calculates his mean percentage success and displays it at the terminal.

9. Write a function ∇ R←INTEGER that requests an entry at the terminal, and verifies if this entry is a valid, integer constant (possibly preceded by a minus sign ‾). If the test is true, the corresponding numerical value is assigned to R, if not a new entry is requested after an error message has been edited.

CHAPTER 6

1. At the beginning of a session, two variables are created:

$R \leftarrow 'TEST'$

$V \leftarrow 3\ 4\ 8$

A function is defined and a request for execution formulated:

(a) $\nabla R \leftarrow MEANA\ V$
  [1] $R \leftarrow (+/V) \div \rho V$
     ∇

   $MEANA\ 2\ 6$

(b) $\nabla R \leftarrow MEANB\ ; V$
  [1] $R \leftarrow (+/V) \div \rho V$
     ∇

   $MEANB$

(c) $\nabla MEANC\ V;R$
  [1] $R \leftarrow (+/V) \div \rho V$
     ∇

   $MEANC\ 2\ 6$

(d) $\nabla MEAND$
  [1] $R \leftarrow (+/V) \div \rho V$
     ∇

   $MEAND$

In each case give the terminal's reply and the values of R and V after execution.

2. Three functions have as headings

$\nabla A \leftarrow B$ *ONE C*

∇ *TWO D;A*

$\nabla B \leftarrow THREE\ D;A$

Specify the types of the variables A, B, C and D (whether they are global or local, and if the latter, which function they belong to):

(*a*) ONE calls TWO. You are interrupted during the execution of TWO.

(*b*) THREE calls TWO. You are interrupted during execution of TWO.

(*c*) ONE calls TWO which calls THREE. You are interrupted during execution of THREE.

3. Write a recursive function to calculate factorial n:

$\nabla R \leftarrow FACT\ N$

4. The polynomial TCHEBYCHEF of degree n is defined by:

$$T_n(x) = \cos(n\ \text{arc}\ \cos x)$$

The value of x of the polynomial of degree n + 1 can be worked out using the recursive formula:

$$T_{n+1}(x) = 2xT_n(x) - T_{n-1}(x)$$

Write a recursive function $\nabla R \leftarrow N$ TCHEB X to perform the calculation.

5. The game of Hanoi towers.

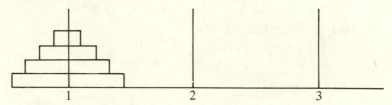

Rings are threaded on to the first pole in descending order of size. The aim of the game is to move all the rings to the third pole, reconstructing an identical figure, using pole 2 if necessary.

The rules are as follows:

The only ring that can be taken from a pole is the one on top. A ring cannot be threaded onto a pole if it is bigger than the ring already on the top.

Write a recursive function which edits at the terminal the successive movements of the rings that will yield the solution.

SOLUTIONS TO EXERCISES

CHAPTER 1

1. ∟ and ×.

2. (*a*) 3
   (*b*) SYNTAX ERROR. The sign ⁻ can only precede a figure.
   (*c*) 3
   (*d*) As for (*b*).

3. (*a*) 4
   (*b*) ⁻7; The interpreter first of all finds the maximum of 7 and 4 before taking the opposite of the result (see the rounding up calculation of Section 1.8).

4. (*a*) Yes.
   (*b*) SYNTAX ERROR. Only the ⁻ sign can appear in an exponent.
   (*c*) Yes.
   (*d*) Yes, as long as a variable E12 has been defined! If not, VALUE ERROR appears.
   (*e*) Yes, the result is 14.5.

5. (*a*) A = ⁻8,   B = ⁻1.
   (*b*) A = ⁻1,   B = ⁻1.
   (*c*) A = 1,   B = 1.
   (*d*) VALUE ERROR appears when instruction 3 is being carried out since the variable A has not been defined.

CHAPTER 2

1. ∗ and !

2. (*a*) Correct.
   (*b*) SYNTAX ERROR: there must be an operand to the right of the sign ×.
   (*c*) SYNTAX ERROR: there must be an function (probably ×) between 5 and A.

(*d*) SYNTAX ERROR: either the closing bracket is missing, or the opening bracket is superfluous.

3. (*a*) 20
   (*b*) 20
   (*c*) 8
   (*d*) 48

4. As it is written, the expression is identical to $x^2 - 2xy - y^2$. Several solutions are possible to obtain the desired result:

   $(X*2) - (2 \times X \times Y) - Y*2$
   $(X*2) + (Y*2) - 2 \times X \times Y$

5. (*a*) Yes.
   (*b*) Yes; the right hand brackets are thus redundant.
   (*c*) No: the result is the value of B^{2-4AC}.
   (*d*) Yes.
   (*e*) No: the result is the value of $B(B-4AC)$.

6. (*a1*) $5 \times (100 \div + /\iota 20) - 6$
   (*b1*) $(+/('\ulcorner * \iota 3) - 1) + 50$
   (*a2*) $5 \times {}^-6 + 100 \div + /\iota 20$
   (*b2*) $50 + + / {}^-1 + '\ulcorner * \iota 3$

7. $P \leftarrow A \times I \times ((1+I)*N) \div {}^-1 + (1+I)*N$ or alternatively
   $P \leftarrow A \times I \times \div /0\ 1 - (1+I)*N$

8. 1.

9. (*a*) $A > B$
   (*b*) $A \leqslant B$
   (*c*) 1

10. (*a*) $3 = +/'X' = TEXT$
    (*b*) $1 \leqslant +/'X' = TEXT$, or $\vee/'X' = TEXT$
    (*c*) $\times/'X' = TEXT$, or $\wedge/'X' = TEXT$

11. (*a*) $X \leftarrow 2 + 8 \times Y < Z$
    (*b*) $X \leftarrow (5 \times Y = Z) + (2 \times Y < Z) + 8 \times Y > Z$, or $X \leftarrow 5 + 3 \times \times Y - Z$

12. There are several solutions. Here is one:

    $1 + (0 > X \times Y) + 2 \times Y < 0$

13. (*a*) $(+/(X-Y)*2)*.5$
    (*b*) $(+/(|X-Y)*P)* \div P$
    (*c*) $\ulcorner/|X-Y$

14. $A \leftarrow (+/R) \div \rho R$
    $G \leftarrow (\times/R)* \div R$
    $H \leftarrow (\rho R) \div +/ \div R$

15. $1++/(X*\iota N)\div!\iota N$, or $1++/\times\backslash X\div\iota N$.

(See the definition of scanning at the end of the manual.)

CHAPTER 3

1. (*a*) *ONE*
   (*b*) *THREE*
   (*c*) *TWO*
   (*d*) When this heading is entered, the system replies with a DEFN ERROR message since it is not valid.
   (*e*) *TWO*
   (*f*) *ONE*
   (*g*) *TWO*

2. (*a*) 4.
   (*b*) 2.
   (*c*) 0, which brings about the exit of the function during execution.
   (*d*) 7.
   (*e*) DOMAIN ERROR: the line number to which there is a branching must be full or empty.

3. (*a*) $\to 0\times\iota\wedge/W>87$.
   (*b*) $\to 27-16\times\vee/'Z'=TEXT$
   (*c*) $\to(17\times 2=\rho\rho TAB)\times\iota 1\neq\rho\rho TAB$

4. (*a1*) Yes.
   (*a2*) Yes.
   (*a3*) Yes; the brackets in (*a1*) and (*a2*) are thus redundant.
   (*a4*) No: the result is ⁻14 instead of 2.
   (*b*)   ∇ *X ANGLE Y*
        [1]   (*X PRODUCT Y*)÷
              ∇   ((*X PRODUCT X*)×*Y PRODUCT Y*)*.5
   (*c1*) ⁻1 2 *ANGLE* 6 4
   (*c2*) ANGLE uses the result of a calculation worked out in the function PRODUCT whose heading indicates that no result would be supplied.
   (*d1*) The function PRODUCT is now defined as having to supply a result of name R. Now, no value was assigned to R in the body of the function.
   (*d2*)   ∇ *R←A PRODUCT B*
        [1] *R←+/A×B*
             ∇
   (*d3*) Yes.

5. The user's active workspace contains 4 objects:
   3 variables (SELLPRICE, COSTPRICE, QUANTITY);
   1 function (PROFIT) whose execution was suspended at line 3.

   (*b1*) The function is exited. If it is to be executed the request must be reformulated.

   (*b2*) Execution is resumed in sequence: execution begins with the third line.

   (*b3*) Execution is resumed beginning with the third line; note that this is exactly what happens with the previous command.

   (*b4*) There is a branching to line number 6357. It is highly unlikely that the function contains as many as 6357 lines; since this line number does not exist, this command has the same effect as the first.

   (*c*) A certain number of lines in the function are executed several times. Amongst them, line 3. Every time this line is encountered the system function □SS instructs that there is an interruption. To make this disappear, type in 3 □RS 'PROFIT'.

   (*d*) Most surprisingly, the system 'loops'. When a set of lines is executed several times, you should always find a test that stops the iterations when a certain condition is satisfied. In this particular instance the test must either be wrong or the condition never reached. Execution of the function must therefore be stopped in order to carry out the necessary corrections. This is done by simply pressing the interruption key BREAK. The computer replies with the line number on which the interruption occurs.

   (*e*) The identifier SELLPRICE has already been assigned to a variable. Two solutions are possible:

   Change the name of the function.
   Destroy the variable SELLPRICE with the command)ERASE.

6.
```
      ∇ R←INSRATE BONUS PERIODS
[1]     REDUC←0
[2]     I←1
[3]     LOOP:REDUC←REDUC+.5+.5×(I≤2)∧INSRATE>.8
[4]     →LOOP×ιPERIOD≥I←I+1
[5]     R←.5⌈INSRATE-REDUC
      ∇
```

REDUC: reduction rate,
   I: period number.

7.
```
      ∇ R←INSRATE PENALTY CLAIMS
[1]     INCR←.1×CLAIMS=1
[2]     INCR←INCR+.4×CLAIMS=2
[3]     INCR←INCR+(CLAIMS-2)×CLAIMS>2
[4]     R←INSRATE+INCR
      ∇
```

INCR: increase rate.

8.
```
     ∇ BONUSPENALTY
[1]    →AFTER×ιACCIDENTS≠0
[2]    YEARS←YEARS+1
[3]    NEWTAX←OLDTAX BONUS YEARS
[4]    →0
[5]   AFTER:YEARS←0
[6]    NEWTAX←OLDTAX PENALTY ACCIDENTS
     ∇
```

9.
```
       ∇MONTECARLO[□]∇
     ∇ A MONTECARLO B
[1]    X←A+(B-A)×(‾1+?1000ρ32001)÷32000
[2]    C←⌈/F X
[3]    Y←C×(‾1+?1000ρ32001)÷32000
[4]    M←+/Y≤F X
[5]    (M÷1000)×C×B-A
     ∇
```

10. (a)
```
     ∇ R←DERIVE X
[1]    R←10000×(F X+1.E‾4)-F X
     ∇
```

(b)
```
     ∇ R←K NEWTON X
[1]    R←X
[2]    LOOP:→END×ι1.E‾4>|F R
[3]    →STOP×ιK=0
[4]    R←R-(F R)÷DERIVE R
[5]    K←K-1
[6]    →LOOP
[7]    END:'THE ALGORITHM CONVERGES'
[8]    →0
[9]    STOP:'THE ALGORITHM DOES NOT CONVERGE'
     ∇
```

CHAPTER 4

1. `4 3ρ'○\|/□/\'`

2. `+/+/M<0`
   `+/,M<0`

3. (a) Numerical vector: 1 2 3

   (b) As in (a).

   (c) As in (a).

   (d) VALUE ERROR unless the variable APL has been defined. If so, the value of this variable is given.

   (e) SYNTAX ERROR: the interpreter is expecting a function to the left of L.

   (f) The character vector APL.

4. `(X/(.5×+/SIDES)-0,SIDES)*.5`

5. 1 whatever the value and structure of this variable.

6. (a) $(R=\lfloor R)/R$
   (b) $(R>(+/R)\div\rho R)/R$
   (c) $\lceil/(R<(+/R)\div\rho R)/R$

7. They have the same value but a different structure. A is a numerical vector with one element, while B is a scalar.

8. (a)
```
      ∇  R←SYMMETRY MAT
[1]      R←∧/∧/MAT=⌽MAT
      ∇
```

(b) LENGTH ERROR in the comparison between the two matrices of different dimensions.

(c)
```
      ∇  R←SYMMETRY MAT
[1]      →NOTSQUARE×ι≠/ρMAT
[2]      R←∧/∧/MAT=⌽MAT
[3]      →0
[4]    NOTSQUARE:R←0
      ∇
```

Conditional statements written in APL are not very easy to read. That is why, on certain systems, a system function has been created called □IF which facilitates writing and comprehension. The syntax of this function is:

⟨*expression*⟩ □IF ⟨*condition*⟩

⟨*condition*⟩ is an APL expression which gives as a result 0 or 1. ⟨*expression*⟩ can be any APL expression, for example a branching which is only executed if the condition is verified (result = 1). Line 1 of the function SYMMETRY can thus be written:

```
[1]    →NOTSQUARE □IF ≠/ρMAT
```

9. $W←{}^{-}1\downarrow(V+1\phi V)\div2.$

10. (a) $V[(V<10)/\iota\rho V]←0$, or more simply $V←V\times V>10.$
    (b) $TEXT[('X'=TEXT)/\iota\rho TEXT]←'Z'$

11. (a) RANK ERROR: A is a scalar and thus dimensionless.
    (b) INDEX ERROR: A is a vector with a single element.
    (c) 2 whatever A.

12. (a) Two possible solutions:

$(N,N)\rho 1,N\rho 0$
$(\iota N)\circ.=\iota N$

(b) $(\iota N)\circ.\geqslant\iota N$

(c) The idea is to multiply a square matrix in which all the rows are equal to V by the identity matrix: $((\iota\rho V)\circ.=\iota\rho V)\times(2\rho\rho V)\rho V.$

(*d*) M is multiplied by the triangular matrix written in (*b*):

$$((\iota\rho V)\circ.\geqslant\iota\rho V)\times M$$

13. The values displayed at the terminal are identical. But:
    (*a*) gives a scalar:
    (*b*) gives a vector of dimension 1;
    (*c*) gives a vector of dimension 1;
    (*d*) gives a matrix of dimensions 1 1.

14. The idea that springs most readily to mind is to generate randomly
    a row index, then a column index, and finally to select the correspond-
    ing element:

    $M[?(\rho M)[1];?(\rho M)[2]]$

    The same result can be obtained more easily by linearising the matrix:

    $(,M)[?\rho,M]$

15. $\nabla SINCOS\ N$
    ```
    [1] ⍂1 2○.○○2×(¯1+⍳N)÷N−1
        ∇
    ```

16. $\nabla PASCAL\ N$
    ```
    [1] ⍂(0,⍳N)∘.!0,⍳N
        ∇
    ```

17.
    ```
        ∇ WORD EXIST DICTIONARY
    [1]    WORD←(ρDICTIONARY)[2]↑WORD
    [2]    ∨/DICTIONARY∧.=WORD
        ∇
    ```

    To enable the inner product of the second line to be correct, the number
    of characters in **WORD** must be equal to the number of columns in
    DICTIONARY. Thus, depending on the particular case, either characters
    should be removed from, or spaces added to **WORD**; this is what line 1
    does.

18.
    ```
        ∇ R←PRIME N
    [1]    R←1
    [2]    LIST←1↓⍳N
    [3]    LOOP:→END×⍳LIST[1]≥N*.5
    [4]    R←R,LIST[1]
    [5]    LIST←(0≠LIST[1]|LIST)/LIST
    [6]    →LOOP
    [7]    END:R←R,LIST
        ∇
    ```

    At each iteration, **R** contains the prime numbers that are already
    known, and **LIST** the residual list for sifting.

19.
```
     ∇ ROMAN DATE
[1]    →ERROR×ι7<⌈/INDEX←'MDCLXVI'ιDATE
[2]    NUMBER←1000 500 100 50 10 5 1[INDEX]
[3]    +/NUMBER×1+¯2×NUMBER<1⌽NUMBER←NUMBER,0
[4]    →0
[5]  ERROR:'INCORRECT DATE'
     ∇
```
Line 1 verifies that DATE is composed of legal characters.
Line 2 calculates NUMBER, a numerical vector in which each
character in DATE is replaced by its arabic value.

20. The result is obtained by indexing CHAIN. The only difficulty lies in
constructing the index matrix.
```
     ∇ TRANSFORM CHAIN
[1]    CHAIN[1+|(ιρCHAIN)∘.-ιρCHAIN]
     ∇
```

CHAPTER 5

1. $(\rho V)=+/V\in 0\ 1$ or $\wedge/A\in 0\ 1$.

2. (a) The value 10 is specified to MAX then displayed at the terminal.
(b) As above.
(c) Printing of the input request □: at the terminal. The value typed in
is assigned to V and its maximum (when it can be calculated), is assigned
to MAX. There is no result displayed at the terminal.
(d) Input request in ⊡. There is no symbol displayed at the terminal.
The value typed in is treated as a string of characters and assigned to V.
Editing of an error message DOMAIN ERROR (the maximum of a string
of characters has no meaning).
(e) Assignment of the value ¯1 to MIN and summation with 1. Display
at the terminal the values ¯1 and 0 one above the other.
(f) The calculations are as above. The values ¯1 and 0 are displayed
side by side.
(g) Input request in □. The symbol □: is printed at the terminal.
If the entry is numerical, it is added to ¯1, the result is assigned to MIN
and the sum of 1 and MIN displayed at the terminal.
(h) Entry request in ⊡. DOMAIN ERROR in the summation of this
entry with 1.

3.
```
     ∇ DEGREE←CONVERT GRAD
[1]    DEGREE←0 60 60⊤GRAD×90×60×60÷100
     ∇
```

4.
```
     ∇ RADIAN←CHANGE DEGREE
[1]    RADIAN←1 60 60⊥DEGREE×○÷180×60×60
     ∇
```

5. Here is a possible solution:

```
∇ R←X POLYNOMIAL COEFFICIENT
[1]   R←+/COEFFICIENT× X*¯1+φ COEFFICIENT
      ∇
```

COEFFICIENT is the vector of the coefficients of the ordered polynomial of increasing powers of x. A more elegant solution is as follows:

```
∇R←X PYNOMIAL COEFFICIENT
[1]   R←X⊥COEFFICIENT∇
```

Take care! COEFFICIENT contains the same values as before, but in the reverse order (with decreasing powers of x).

6.
```
      ∇ R←E1 INTER E2
[1]     E1←,E1
[2]     R←(E1∊E2)/E1
      ∇
```

7.
```
      ∇ R←E1 UNION E2
[1]     E1←,E1
[2]     E2←,E2
[3]     R←E1,(~E2∊E1)/E2
      ∇
```

8.
```
      ∇ CANNON
[1]     SHOTS←TARGETS←0
[2]    DISTANCE:D←999+?6501
[3]     'DISTANCE OF THE TARGET : ',(▼D),' METRES'
[4]    ATTEMPT:SHOTS←SHOTS+1
[5]     'SET THE SIGTH PLEASE (DECIMAL DEGREES)'
[6]     ALPHA←⎕
[7]     X←7500×1○ALPHA÷90
[8]     →(SHORT,HIT,LONG)[2+(×X-D)×50<|X-D]
[9]    SHORT:'SHOT TOO SHORT BY: ',(▼D-X),' METRES'
[10]    →ATTEMPT
[11]   LONG:'SHOT TOO LONG BY : ',(▼X-D),' METRES'
[12]    →ATTEMPT
[13]   HIT:TARGETS←TARGETS+1
[14]    'FIRE'
[15]    'DO YOU WANT ANOTHER TARGET (Y/N) ? '
[16]    →DISTANCE ⎕IF 'Y'=1↑⍞
[17]    'PERCENTAGE SUCCESS : ',▼100×TARGETS÷SHOTS
      ∇
```

TARGETS: number of targets reached;

SHOTS: number of shots fired;

⎕IF: see the solution to exercise 8 in chapter 4.

```
9.      ∇ R←INTEGER
   [1]    REQUEST:ENTRY←⎕
   [2]     →ERROR×ι~∧/ENTRY∊'¯1234567890'
   [3]     →(CORRECT,TEST,ERROR)[1+2⌊+/ENTRY='¯']
   [4]   ERROR:'INCORRECT ENTRY'
   [5]     →REQUEST
   [6]   TEST:→ERROR×ι'¯'≠1↑ENTRY
   [7]   CORRECT:R←⍎ENTRY
        ∇
```

Line 2: test of the validity of the characters in ENTRY.

Line 3: if in ENTRY the number of signs '¯' = 0 the input is correct; if >1 it is incorrect; if =1 it is correct as long as it is placed at the beginning (line 6).

CHAPTER 6

1. (a) The result 4 is displayed at the terminal. After execution R = 'TEST' and V = 3 4 8.

   (b) The execution request brings about a **VALUE ERROR** on V which is now a local variable; in fact it has been used in a calculation without having been previously defined.

   (c) There is no result displayed at the terminal. After execution R = 'TEST' and V = 3 4 8.

   (d) There is no result displayed at the terminal. After execution R = 5 and V = 3 4 8.

2. (a) A is local to ONE;
   B is local to TWO;
   C is local to ONE;
   D is local to TWO.

   (b) A is local to ONE;
   B is local to ONE;
   C is global;
   D is local to TWO.

   (c) A is local to ONE;
   B is local to THREE;
   C is local to ONE;
   D is local to THREE.

3.
```
        ∇ R←FACT N
   [1]    →ZERO×ιN=0
   [2]    R←N×FACT N-1
   [3]    →0
   [4]   ZERO:R←1
        ∇
```

4.
```
     ∇ R←N  TCHEB  X
[1]    →ZERO×ιN=0
[2]    →UN×ιN=1
[3]    R←(2×X×(N-1)TCHEB  X)-(N-2)TCHEB  X
[4]    →0
[5]  ZERO:R←1
[6]    →0
[7]  UN:R←X
     ∇
```

5. The principle of recursion is as follows: to move n rings from the first
pole X to the last pole Y, all that needs to be done is to move the first
n−1 rings from X to the intermediate pole Z, then the remaining one
from X to Y, and finally to move the n−1 rings on Z to Y.

If we know how to solve the problem for n−1 rings, we can solve it for
n. Now the solution for n=1 is trivial. This principle enables us to find
the solution for each value of n.

In principle the function has 3 arguments:

N: number of rings to be moved;

X: number on the first pole;

Y: number on the final pole.

To write it in its dyadic form, we regroup the last two in the vector
NUMBER.

```
     ∇ N  HANOI  NUMBER;INTER
[1]    →MOVE×ιN=1
[2]    INTER←6-+/NUMBER
[3]    (N-1)HANOI  NUMBER[1],INTER
[4]    1 HANOI  NUMBER
[5]    (N-1)HANOI  INTER,NUMBER[2]
[6]    →0
[7]  MOVE:'MOVE  ONE  RING  FROM  POLE
     ∇          ';NUMBER[1];'  TO  POLE  ';NUMBER[2]
```

INTER is the number of the intermediate pole; this variable must be
made local so that **HANOI** functions correctly.

APPENDIX 1

APL ALPHABET

Here is the list of characters available on an APL terminal.

Letters

A B C D E F G H I J K L M N O P Q R S T U V W X Y Z △ (delta)

Figures		>	greater than
0 1 2 3 4 5 6 7 8 9		≠	not equal to
Other symbols		α	alpha
	space	∈	epsilon
[	left bracket	ι	iota
]	right bracket	ρ	rho
(	left parenthesis	ω	omega
)	right parenthesis	:	colon
;	semi colon	|	stile
/	slash	,	comma
\	back slash	⊥	base
←	left arrow	⊤	top
→	right arrow	○	circle
+	plus	?	question mark
−	minus	~	tilde
×	times	↑	up arrow
÷	divide	↓	down arrow
*	star	⊂	open shoe
⌈	upstile	⊃	close shoe
⌊	downstile	∩	cap
∧	and	∪	cup
∨	or	_	underscore
<	less than	○	null
≤	less than or equal to	□	quad
=	equal to	.	dot
≥	greater than or equal to	‾	overbar

'	quote	$	dollar
∇	del	◇	diamond
¨	dieresis	{	open brace
⊢	left tack	}	close brace
⊣	right tack		

Composite symbols

Other APL symbols are obtained by superimposing two characters:
type in one of the characters, backspace, then type in the other
character. Here is a list of the most commonly occurring ones.

! (. ')	quote dot	⊖ (○ -)	circle bar
φ (○ ǀ)	phi	⌿ (/ —)	slash bar /[□IO]
⍉ (○ \)	transpose	⍀ (\ —)	slope bar \[□IO]
I (⊥ T)	I-beam	⍙ (⊥ ○)	base null
⍞ (□ ')	quote quad	⍢ (T °)	top null
⍟ (○ *)	log	⍋ (△ ǀ)	delta stile
⍲ (~ ∧)	nand	⍖ (▽ǀ)	del stile
⍱ (~ ∨)	nor	⍫ (∇ ~)	del tilde
⍝ (∩ °)	cap hull	⍒ (OUT)	out

Similarly, the alphabetic characters can be underscored, which gives
new letters:

A B C D E F G H I J K L M N O P Q R S T U V W X Y Z △

APPENDIX 2

DYADIC SCALAR FUNCTIONS

Dyadic scalar functions can be applied to two expressions of the same dimensions, or to a scalar and an expression of any dimension.

	Symbol	Meaning	Examples
ARITHMETIC	$A + B$	Addition of A to B	$10\ ^-2 + 21\ 5 \rightarrow 31\ 3$
	$A - B$	Subtraction of B from A	$10\ ^-2 - 9\ 5 \rightarrow 1\ ^-7$
	$A \times B$	Multiplication of A by B	$^-5\ 2 \times 3\ 5 \rightarrow\ ^-15\ 10$
	$A \div B$	Division of A by B	$10\ 4 \div 5\ 8 \rightarrow 2\ 0.5$
	$A * B$	A to the power B	$2\ ^-3 * 3\ 2 \rightarrow 8\ 9$
	$A \circledast B$	Logarithm to base A of B	$10\ 4 \circledast 10\ 16 \rightarrow 1\ 2$
	$A \ulcorner B$	Maximum of A and B	$10\ ^-2 \ulcorner 21\ ^-5 \rightarrow 21\ ^-2$
	$A \llcorner B$	Minimum of A and B	$10\ ^-2 \llcorner 21\ ^-5 \rightarrow 10\ ^-5$
	$A\ !\ B$	Binomial coefficient C_B^A	$2\ 4!4\ 4 \rightarrow 6\ 1$
	$A\ \vert\ B$	A residue B; if $A \ne 0$: residue of $B \div A$ if $A = 0$: value of B	$0\ 5\vert 8\ 9 \rightarrow 8\ 4$
COMPARATIVE	$A < B$	The result is 1 if the relation	$5\ 9 < 2\ 9 \rightarrow 0\ 0$
	$A \leqslant B$	is true, 0 if the relation is	$5\ 9 \leqslant 2\ 9 \rightarrow 0\ 1$
	$A = B$	false.	$5\ 9 = 2\ 9 \rightarrow 0\ 1$
	$A \geqslant B$		$5\ 9 \geqslant 2\ 9 \rightarrow 1\ 1$
	$A > B$		$5\ 9 > 2\ 9 \rightarrow 1\ 0$
	$A \ne B$		$5\ 9 \ne 2\ 9 \rightarrow 1\ 0$
		$=$ and $\ne$ can also operate on characters	$'AB' = 'AC' \rightarrow 1\ 0$ $'AB' \ne 'AC' \rightarrow 0\ 1$

			A B	$A \lor B$	$A \land B$	$A \barvee B$	$A \barwedge B$
LOGICAL	$A \lor B$	A OR (inclusive) B	0 0	0	0	1	1
	$A \land B$	A AND B	0 1	1	0	0	1
	$A \barvee B$	A NOR B	1 0	1	0	0	1
	$A \barwedge B$	A NAND B	1 1	1	1	0	0

Circular functions (B in radians) and hyperbolics of B

TRIGONOMETRIC

$A \circ B$

$0 \circ B$ $(1-B*2)*0.5$	
$1 \circ B$ *sin B*	$^{-}1 \circ B$ *Arcsin B*
$2 \circ B$ *cos B*	$^{-}2 \circ B$ *Arccos B*
$3 \circ B$ *tan B*	$^{-}3 \circ B$ *Arctan B*
$4 \circ B$ $(1+B*2)*.5$	$^{-}4 \circ B$ $(^{-}1+B*2)*.5$
$5 \circ B$ *sinh B*	$^{-}5 \circ B$ *Arcsinh B*
$6 \circ B$ *cosh B*	$^{-}6 \circ B$ *Arccosh B*
$7 \circ B$ *tanh B*	$^{-}7 \circ B$ *Arctanh B*

MONADIC SCALAR FUNCTIONS

Monadic scalar functions can be applied to expressions of any
dimension – to each element of them.

Symbol	Meaning	Examples
$+ A$	*Identity*	$+ 10 \ ^{-}2\ 0 \rightarrow 10 \ ^{-}2\ 0$
$- A$	*Negation*	$- 10 \ ^{-}2\ 0 \rightarrow\ ^{-}10\ 2\ 0$
$\times A$	*Signum of A*	$\times 10 \ ^{-}2\ 0 \rightarrow 1 \ ^{-}1\ 0$
$\div A$	*Reciprocal of A*	$\div 10 \ ^{-}2 \rightarrow 0.1 \ ^{-}0.5$
$* A$	*Exponential of A*	$* 1 \qquad \rightarrow 2.7182818$
$\circledast A$	*Naperian log of A*	$\circledast 10 \qquad \rightarrow 2.3025851$
$\lceil A$	*Rounding up*	$\lceil 10.5 \ ^{-}2.1 \rightarrow 11 \ ^{-}2$
$\lfloor A$	*Rounding down*	$\lfloor 10.5 \ ^{-}2.1 \rightarrow 10 \ ^{-}3$
$! A$	*Factorial of A*	$!6\ 1\ 0 \qquad \rightarrow 720\ 1\ 1$
$\circ? A$	*Pi times A*	$\circ 2 \qquad \rightarrow 6.2831853$
$\sim A$	*NOT A . (Boolean A)*	$\sim 1\ 0\ 0\ 1 \rightarrow 0\ 1\ 1\ 0$
$? A$	*Random integer of ιA†*	$? 10\ 20\ 9 \rightarrow 7\ 17\ 2$

OPERATORS

The letters f and g represent two dyadic functions of any type.

Symbol	Meaning	Examples
f / [I] A	Reduction of A by f along the Ith dimension†	$+/[1]\begin{matrix}1\ 2\ 3\\4\ 5\ 6\end{matrix} \rightarrow 5\ 7\ 9$
f \ [I] A	Scan of A by f along the Ith dimension†	$+\backslash[2]\begin{matrix}1\ 2\ 3\\4\ 5\ 6\end{matrix} \rightarrow \begin{matrix}1\ 3\ 6\\4\ 9\ 15\end{matrix}$
A ∘ . f B	Outer product of A and B by f	$2\ 3\ \circ .\times\ 4\ 1 \rightarrow \begin{matrix}8\ \ 2\\12\ 3\end{matrix}$
A f . g B	Inner product of A and B by f and g. (+ . × matrix product)	$\begin{matrix}2\ 3\\1\ 2\\4\ 1\end{matrix} +.\times\ \begin{matrix}1\ 4\\2\ 3\end{matrix} \rightarrow \begin{matrix}8\ 17\\5\ 10\\6\ 19\end{matrix}$

Note that: f / and f \ apply to the last dimension,
f ⌿ and f ⍀ apply to the first dimension.

† *The results depend on the index origin (0 or 1)*

Special characters
The characters:

⌿ ⍀ ⍢ ⍙ ⍋ ⍒ ⊖ ⍟ ⌹ ⊟ ⍤ ⍕ ⍱ ⍲ ! ⍥

are obtained by superimposing:

— — ~ ~ ∘ ∘ ∘ ∘ □ □ ∘ ∘ | | ' ∘
/ \ ∨ ∧ \ | - * ' ÷ ⊥ ⊤ ∇ ∆ . ∩

MIXED FUNCTIONS

In the following examples, M is the array $\begin{matrix}5\ 2\ 8\\3\ 1\ 2\end{matrix}$ and V is the vector
2 9 1 3 9 5.

Symbol	Meaning	Examples
ρ B	Dimension of B	$\rho\ M \rightarrow 2\ 3$
A ρ B	Restructure of B to the dimensions A	$2\ 4\rho V \rightarrow \begin{matrix}2\ 9\ 1\ 3\\9\ 5\ 2\ 9\end{matrix}$
ι B	Vector of B prime integers†	$\iota\ 3 \rightarrow 1\ 2\ 3$

$A \iota B$	Finding B in A†	$V \iota M \to \begin{matrix} 6\ 1\ 7 \\ 4\ 3\ 1 \end{matrix}$
$A \in B$	A is a member of B	$2\ 4 \in M \to 1\ 0$
$, B$	Ravelling B	$, M \to 5\ 2\ 8\ 3\ 1\ 2$
$A, [I]\ B$	Catenation of A to B following the Ith dimension.† If I is not an integer then lamination	$M, [2]\ 9\ 2 \to \begin{matrix} 5\ 2\ 8\ 9 \\ 3\ 1\ 2\ 2 \end{matrix}$
$A \uparrow B$ $A \downarrow B$	Take (or drop) |A elements of B: if $A \geqslant 0$: from the beginning, if $A \leqslant 0$: from the end	$1\ ^-2 \uparrow M \to 2\ 8$ $2 \downarrow V \to 1\ 3\ 9\ 5$
$\triangle B$ $\triangledown B$	Ascending (or descending) sort. Sorted indices of B†	$\triangle V \to 3\ 1\ 4\ 6\ 2\ 5$ $\triangledown V \to 2\ 5\ 6\ 4\ 1\ 3$
$\phi\ [I]\ B$	Reversion of B on the Ith dimension†	$\phi[1]M \to \begin{matrix} 3\ 1\ 2 \\ 5\ 2\ 8 \end{matrix}$
$A\ \phi\ [I]\ B$	Rotation of |A elements of B following the Ith dimension†	$1\ 2\phi M \to \begin{matrix} 2\ 8\ 5 \\ 2\ 3\ 1 \end{matrix}$
$\varnothing B$ $A \varnothing B$	Transposition of B Transposition of B by A	$1\ 1\varnothing M \to 5\ 1$
$A\ /\ [I]\ B$	Compression of B by A along the Ith dimension†	$1\ 0\ 1/M \to \begin{matrix} 5\ 8 \\ 3\ 2 \\ 5\ 2\ 8 \end{matrix}$
$A \setminus [I]\ B$	Expansion of B by A along the Ith dimension†	$1\ 0\ 1 \backslash M \to \begin{matrix} 0\ 0\ 0 \\ 3\ 1\ 2 \end{matrix}$
$A\ ?\ B$	Different, random elements of A taken in ιB†	$3\ ?\ 9 \to 4\ 7\ 1$
$A \top B$	Encoding B in base A	$10\ 10\top 25 \to 2\ 5$
$A \perp B$	Decoding B written in base A	$10\ 10\perp 2\ 5 \to 25$
$\boxplus B$	Inversion of the matrix B	$\boxplus \begin{matrix} 2\ 1 \\ 4\ 1 \end{matrix} \to \begin{matrix} 0.5\ 0.5 \\ 2\ \ ^-1 \end{matrix}$
$A \boxplus B$	Solution of the linear system B: matrix of coefficients, A: second member	$6\ 2\boxplus \begin{matrix} 2\ 1 \\ 4\ 1 \end{matrix} \to\ ^-2\ 10$

Note that: $, \phi / \backslash$ *apply to the last dimension,*
$\quad\quad\quad \ominus \nearrow \diagdown$ *apply to the first dimension.*

† *The results depend on the index origin (0 or 1).*

DEFINITION AND MODIFICATION OF FUNCTIONS

The symbol ∇ followed by the function heading switches the system to modification mode. To return to execution mode the symbol ∇ must be retyped.

 ∇ *FUNC*
[4]

To create a function the symbol ∇ followed by the function heading must be entered: a heading defines the function name (MEAN), argument or arguments (X), eventual result (R), possible local variables (SUM). There are six types of headings:

 ∇ $R \leftarrow MEAN\ X\ ;SUM$
[1] $SUM \leftarrow +/\ X$
[2] $R \leftarrow SUM \div \rho X$
[3]
  ∇

Arguments	Without result	With result
0 → *niladic*	∇ *FUNC*	∇ $R \leftarrow FUNC$
1 → *monadic*	∇ *FUNC B*	∇ $R \leftarrow FUNC\ B$
2 → *dyadic*	∇ *A FUNC B*	∇ $R \leftarrow A\ FUNC\ B$

A line can be referenced by a label (LA): [5] LA:I←1.
The heading names and the labels are local.

Command	Meaning
[□]	*Printing of the function*
[N□]	*Printing line N of the function*
[□P]	*Printing from line P onwards of the function*
[N P□]	*Printing lines N to P of the function*
[N□P]	*Modification of line N of the function*
[N↓]	*Deletion of line N of the function*
[N P↓]	*Deletion of lines N to P of the function*

OTHER OPERATORS

Symbol	Meaning

$\rightarrow B$	Branches to:
	    if B valid line number: branch to this line
	    if B not valid line number: exit from the function
	    if B empty vector: continue in sequence on the next line

$\pounds\, B$	*Execution of alphanumeric expressions:* $\pounds'1+2'$
$\top B$	*Conversion of numeric array to character array*
$A \top B$	*Same usage, but following the format of A*
$\square \leftarrow B$	*Printing of the value B (quad)*
$B \leftarrow \square$	*Entry request: execution then specification of result*
$\square \leftarrow B$	*Printing of the value B without carriage return (quote-quad)*
$B \leftarrow$	*Alphanumeric entry request; specification of the string*
$A \leftarrow B$	*Assignment of the value B to the variable A*

SYSTEM FUNCTIONS AND VARIABLES

Symbol	Meaning
	One can consult or modify their value; their rounded down value is written in square brackets, which is universally recognised.

□ *CT*	*Deviation allowed in comparisons (comparison tolerance)*
□ *LX*	*Latent expression (executed at the time of a)LOAD . ['']*
□ *IO*	*Index origin (0 or 1)* [1]
□ *PP*	*Maximum number of figures for printing (printing precision)*
□ *PW*	*Maximum width of printing , in characters (printing width)*
□ *RL*	*Root of the next random number (random link)*

Functions

□ *AI*	*Accounting information*
□ *AV*	*Vector of the 256 APL characters*
□ *CR*	*Canonic representation of a function*
□ *DL*	*Delay*
□ *EX*	*Erase variables or functions under program control (expunge)*
□ *FI*	*Conversion of character chain to numeric chain*
□ *FMT*	*Format function*
□ *FX*	*Establishment of a function*
□ *IF*	*Conditional expression*
□ *LC*	*Line number during execution*
□ *NC*	*Name classification*
□ *NL*	*List of APL objects*
□ *QS*	*List of lines stopped in a function*
□ *QT*	*List of lines traced in a function*
□ *RS*	*Deletion of the stopping of a function*
□ *RT*	*Deletion of the trace of a function*
□ *SS*	*Stopping a function*
□ *ST*	*Trace of a function*
□ *TS*	*Date, time (year, month, day, hour, minute, second)*
□ *TT*	*Terminal type*
□ *UI*	*User's name*
□ *UL*	*Number of terminals connected*
□ *VI*	*Validity of a character chain*
□ *WA*	*Number of free bytes (multiples of 8 bits) in a workspace*

OTHER SYMBOLS

∇	*Beginning and end of a function definition (carrot)*
'	*Boundary of string of characters (quote) . 'TOTO'*
⋒	*Comment*
( )	*Modification of the evaluation order of an expression*
[ ]	*Indexation of variables or operators*
→	*To exit from the function in execution and all functions called with it; interruption of an entry request in □*
⍤	*Interruption of an entry request in ⍞ (superposition of the characters O U T).*
;	*Separates expressions, indices, local variables*

SYSTEM COMMANDS

The following abbreviations have been adopted below:

iden: *identifier of the work block sometimes preceded by the sign-on number of its owner.*

key: *alphanumeric password which protects access to a work block or a sign-on number.*

name(s): *list of the names of APL objects (variables or functions) separated by at least one space. Those named in square brackets are optional.*

MANAGEMENT OF WORKSPACE

)LOAD iden [:key]   *Loading of a workspace, the contents of the active space is lost*

)COPY iden [:key] [names]   *Copying of APL objects in the active space or of the whole space if names are omitted*

)PCOPY iden [:key] [names]   *Same use, but the objects of the active space are protected in the case of a duplication of names*

)SAVE [iden] [:key]   *Save the active block under the name iden, sometimes with a password*

)DROP iden [:key]   *Destruction of a workspace in the library*

)LIB NNNN   *List of workspaces in the library under the sign-on number NNNN*

)WSID [iden]   *Name of the active workspace or modification of its name*

MANAGEMENT OF OBJECTS IN THE ACTIVE SPACE

)FNS [letter] [letter]	List of functions (from the letter indicated up to the other indicated letter)
)VARS [letter] [letter]	List of variables (from the letter indicated up to the other indicated letter)
)ERASE names	Destruction of the objects indicated (the functions should not be interrupted)
)CLEAR	Clearing the whole of the active space including its name

CONTROL OF THE ACTIVE SPACE

)ORIGIN [0 or 1]	Index origin or modification of this origin
)DIGITS [1 to 16]	Maximum number of figures for printing, or modification of this number
)WIDTH [30 to 133]	Maximum width of printed line or modification of this width
)SI	List of suspended functions
)SINL	List of suspended variables and their associated local variables
)SIC	Exit all the suspended functions and the functions called with them

INDEX